This Booklet is provided to you by
Dying With Dignity
55 Eglinton Ave East Suite 802
Toronto, ON M4P 1G8
www.dyingwithdignity.ca
416 486 3998 or 1 800 495 6156

Breathe

Breathe

Gary Hyndman

Cotton & Cigars Publishing, LLC
Greenville, SC

Published by Cotton & Cigars Publishing, LLC
Greenville, SC

Breathe
Copyright©2005 by Cotton & Cigars Publishing, LLC
ISBN: 0-9761982-0-7
Library of Congress: 2004113334

10   9   8   7   6   5   4   3   2   1

*To Barbara and Brian who embodied for me
what it means to live courageously in this tenuous world.*

"The miracle is not to walk on water.
The miracle is to walk on the green earth,
dwelling deeply in the present moment
and feeling truly alive."

Thich Nhat Hanh

Acknowledgements

While writing is very much a solitary experience, publishing a book is anything but. The effort to bring this story to print represents the collective effort of a team of people to whom I am most grateful.

I wish to thank Doris and Leon Galloway, without whose moral and financial support this project could never have been realized; Sam Rhodes, upon whose vision it was carried forward; my editor Sandy Richardson, for her kind and patient tutelage; Kathy Vass and Ben Muldrow for their marketing expertise; my wife, Susan, who endured mostly without complaint the evenings, weekends and even holidays I was preoccupied with my writing; and all the good people who charitably read rough drafts of the text and offered critiques—some of which were not flattering—that ultimately helped shape this into a stronger piece of literature.

Prologue

In the spring of 1993, I answered the phone in my study at the Unitarian Universalist Church of Spartanburg, South Carolina, where I served as minister at the time, only to find that by the time I returned the receiver to its cradle, my life was already shifting in a new direction.

The caller identified herself as Barbara Baco. She and her quadriplegic son, Brian, needed immediate help. She explained that on weekday mornings a nursing assistant came to their home to help her transfer Brian from his bed into his wheelchair. The assistant also helped return him to his bed each evening.

But insurance coverage did not reimburse the family for professional care on weekends, so Barbara had been forced to turn instead to friends to help her negotiate the tricky transfer process each Saturday and Sunday. In the period immediately following Brian's injury, friends and family had stepped in to lend a hand. But as the seventh anniversary of his accident approached, volunteers for that assignment had grown scarce, leaving Brian to face the unhappy prospect of being confined to his bed from Friday night until Monday morning each week.

Barbara's phone call was an appeal to our congregation for some weekend help. That she resorted to seeking the kindness of strangers demonstrated the magnitude of her desperation. Asked to explain what drew her to our church, she could only say that she had heard about us and had "a sense" we would be sympathetic.

I agreed to place an announcement in the church newsletter appealing for volunteers. But as I jotted down Barbara's phone number and address, the gesture seemed mostly obligatory, carried out without any real expectation her cause would attract any takers. With only about 140 members, our congregation was already plagued with more volunteer assignments than volunteers. Though the Bacos' plight seemed very real, it was hard to generate much enthusiasm when I was already wrestling with a series of organizational holes to fill, each one worthy in its own right.

But when Barbara dictated directions to her house, a shudder of recognition ran through me. The location she pinpointed in a community of many square miles was to be found but a single block from an apartment that was to become my new home just two weeks later.

Barbara's request for help never found its way into the church newsletter. Within days, I called her back and volunteered myself for what seemed a very small act of kindness, little knowing all that it stood to teach me.

Four times each weekend I made the short walk to the small, uninspiring house on White Oak Street. The exterior of the Baco residence seemed as tired as its inhabitants. Nothing in my professional training or experience had prepared me for the dismal circumstances I discovered there—a severely disabled and bloated young man nearly twenty-three years old, living with his divorced, middle-aged mother. A huge, metallic hospital bed dominated the tiny living room, symbolic of the degree to which Brian's disability had come to dominate that family's life.

I was soon to learn that transferring Brian from the bed into his wheelchair each Saturday and Sunday morning and returning him each evening created considerable anxiety for them. Despite the fact that over the last seven years, they had completed this procedure thousands of times, I never saw either mother or son approach it casually. For the seconds it took to settle him into his chair or bed, Brian would be disconnected from the respirator that served as his lifeline.

The routine went like this: A lift with a metal arm suspended from its base was wheeled into place at the side of Brian's bed and straps were wrapped around his torso and legs. The straps, in turn, were secured to hooks on the lift arm. Next, Barbara turned the lift's crank until Brian's body was elevated above the mattress. With Barbara supporting his head, I was assigned to hold Brian's legs. Then, she disconnected the tube at his throat that supplied oxygen from the respirator to his trachea, initiating the critical transfer process. Moving swiftly in concert, we wheeled the lift supporting all 200-something pounds of Brian's unresponsive body and deposited him into his chair.

Each evening the process was reversed. Once Barbara reconnected him to the respirator beside his bed or the portable unit attached to his wheelchair, and the straps were removed, both she and Brian visibly relaxed. With my contribution complete, I was free either to excuse myself or to remain for a visit.

While I sometimes stayed for a chat, it would be inaccurate to say our relationship ever developed into a friendship. Besides my general discomfort with Brian's condition, there was too little history and too much space between us for much of a bond to form. Most of our conversations felt forced, more a way to fill the awkward silences than spontaneous exchanges between close friends. Ours was a business partnership defined by mutual self-interest. I provided a necessary service for which he was politely appreciative. He, on the other hand, provided me an opportunity to be of service for which I was equally grateful. There was never any indication from Brian that he wanted it to be any more than that.

But over the next six months the Bacos' lives came to converge with my own. And with the help of Brian, Barbara, and interviews with family and friends, a dramatic story began to unfold, one that demanded to be told. It is a story as poignant for its courage as its misery.

Chapter 1

Barbara Baco, who was adopted as a young girl, attempted as an adult to establish contact with her birth mother. But her overtures were spurned. The identity of her biological father remains a mystery to this day, though she suspects he was a relative of her adoptive family. Her adoptive father, the one true, consistently caring figure in her life, abandoned her in a different way by his premature death.

Thus, there was a certain psychic symmetry in Barbara's choice of Herman Baco as her husband, a man she describes as emotionally distant. Her temper still flares at the memory early in their marriage when she announced her intention to go fishing with her brother and his wife. Herman responded by casually asking who she had found to keep their infant son, Brian.

According to Barbara, the incident reflected the limitations of the marriage. The brunt of the care for Brian and his younger brother Dean fell disproportionately on her shoulders, she says. Apart from his participation in the children's athletic activities, Herman was largely emotionally absent as a husband and father.

That dynamic set the stage for a slowly hemorrhaging relationship, with Herman's perpetual distance matched by Barbara's festering resentment. A last gasp stab at marriage counseling could not rekindle whatever good will had once existed between them.

The summer of Brian's twelfth birthday, the Bacos and their two sons vacationed at Disney World. That week in Florida was to be their last official act as an intact family. On returning to Spartanburg, Barbara announced her intention to leave Herman, effectively ending their seventeen years of marriage.

Shortly thereafter, she left the family home and set up housekeeping in a tiny, nearby apartment. In family counseling, the Bacos agreed it would be less disruptive for their sons to remain in the familiar surroundings of their father's home. The marriage may have fallen far short of expectations, but Barbara and Herman refused to make matters worse by putting their children in the middle of their own unhappiness. Where Brian and Dean were concerned, they initially worked hard to present a united front as parents.

The boys reacted to the news of their parents' breakup in their characteristic, individual fashion. Brian remained stoic and seemingly unfazed, while his younger brother Dean grew angry and defiant, even accusing his mother of abandonment.

As happens in families, the Baco brothers were typecast early in life with well-defined roles. Brian, as the older son, assumed the title of the accomplished child while Dean accepted the less prestigious but equally demanding role of the problem child. And consistent with family expectations, whatever Brian did well, Dean set out with equal aplomb to screw up.

According to Barbara, Brian arrived in the world with a mischievous streak. After his birth, she bought him a ceramic piggy bank to encourage him to save his money. But at an early age, he hammered the piggybank into pieces to get to the change inside.

There was also the incident of the miniature rocking chair Barbara's mother gave her for her second birthday. It became a familiar furnishing in Barbara's childhood bedroom and grew into a keepsake she cherished for its sentimental value. After Brian and Dean were born, she had the chair refinished with the idea of passing it down as a family heirloom.

"Then, one day for some insane reason," she recalls, "Brian and Dean busted it up. I was so angry."

So angry, in fact, that she locked herself in the bathroom and refused appeals from her sons to come out. She eventually took the remains of the prized rocking chair and burned them unceremoniously in the family woodstove.

Brian's childhood friend Mike Burnette attests to his mischievous streak as well. Mike met Brian and Dean after his father cleared brush from a power company right-of-way that had separated their homes. The boys happily discovered they all went to the same Catholic school. The friendship between Mike and Brian was cemented playing baseball and soccer on the newly cleared field and the fantasy board game Dungeons and Dragons at the picnic table in Mike's backyard.

Their activities were often guided by Brian's irrepressible nature. One day the boys purchased a package of bottle rockets and set them off in a garden hose and up the family chimney. Brian taunted Dean, chasing his younger brother around the house wielding the fireworks as a weapon. When Dean tried to hide in the bedroom, Brian cracked the door and lit a bottle rocket that took off like a torpedo across the room. As Dean howled, Brian and Mike doubled over laughing.

Mike, who was a naturally cautious youth, was fascinated by his friend's love of schoolboy pranks. Mike conscientiously paid his admission to the school football games while Brain scaled the fence to get in free. He watched as Brian gleefully coated a rival's car with spray from a fire extinguisher. It was at Brian's urging that Mike rode his first roller coaster at an amusement park and Brian who coaxed him into sipping his first beer.

Another friend, David Cullen, also remembers Brian as a prankster, but one with a conscience. David says he was drawn to Brian because of his intelligence and sense of humor, a combination he found lacking in most of his peers. He describes him as possessing a "rapier wit" capable of dissecting pretense. But he adds that his friend used this formidable gift with care. Though prone to needle people he thought deserving of it, he was no bully.

"He was not inclined to go after people who could not defend themselves," says David.

The boys first met in junior high school and quickly became friends as well as scholastic rivals. Barbara says that after Brian scored an impressive 1310 on the SAT, he was annoyed to learn that David scored even higher.

But they were aligned in their boredom with school. With their social studies teacher napping at the front of the classroom, Brian and David found ways to entertain themselves besides studying.

"We had these epic spitball wars," David says.

They eventually graduated to making pin darts out of a sewing needle that was pushed through the capped end of a shoestring. The darts were loaded into a drinking straw and fired at each other with the goal of inflicting pain.

In a ninth grade German class, David remembers how Brian and another student, Stephen Echols, engaged in a sadistic ritual of punching each other.

"Basically, it was an excuse to hit each other in the arm as hard as they could," he says. "Any wince indicated you were a wimp."

David contends the clowning around was not idle activity; rather, it was designed to cope with an educational system determined to regiment them and dull their wonder with life. The emphasis on rote memorization of facts failed to satisfy their need to think for themselves. So, Brian, David, and Mike all turned to fantasy novels as an outlet for their vivid imaginations. The fantasies grew into their textbooks, which they read, digested, and traded among themselves as students of an alternative curriculum.

From an early age, athletics played a prominent role in Brian's life. Beginning with swimming, where he collected a drawer full of ribbons, competition seemed to bring out the best in him. But it was to be on the soccer field that he would truly distinguish himself. His natural quickness and grace were well suited to a sport that rewards both.

His elite youth league soccer coach, Gabe Volk, says Brian was an integral member of his teams that won four state championships in their division. As a freshman Brian made the high school soccer team, becoming one of the youngest persons in school history to earn that distinction. Volk predicts that he eventually would have earned a scholarship to play soccer at the collegiate level.

But Brian's achievements were not limited to sports. In the classroom, straight A's were the norm, earning him membership in the school's Beta Club. What impressed people most was the seeming ease with which he managed academic excellence, a fact he attributed to paying careful attention in class. It was that knack for being able to absorb a large block of information and recall it on command that set him apart from most of his peers.

David, who was bested regularly by Brian in chess matches, still marvels at his friend's uncanny recollection of chess strategies. But Brian was equally adept at supplying answers to questions in Jeopardy, Trivial Pursuit, or any other game that rewards a good memory. It was no surprise, then, that he scored near the genius level on an intelligence test.

David also admired Brian for his honesty. "If you asked him a question, he wouldn't give you a bunch of bullshit," he says.

There was also a serious side to Brian that was never satisfied with superficial consideration of a topic. "He was a thinker," says Mike. "He was always a thinker."

The two boys spent many nights sleeping over at each other's homes, sitting up until early morning talking endlessly about sports, religion, politics, science, social issues, and a future that burned bright.

"We could have intellectual discussions where other kids our age didn't," Mike recalls.

At school, this lanky, affable kid with the razor-sharp wit moved easily among a diverse group of students. At one time, his inner circle of friends included the brilliant but geeky David, straight-laced Mike and Paul Choberka, whose ambition, according to Mike, was to be popular.

"Brian was someone who was accepting of a lot of different people," says Mike. "He appreciated a lot of things other high school kids overlooked."

Adults perceived him as a polite and responsible young man—just the kind of person they wanted their children to grow up to be. And for his parents, Brian was the perennial good boy who presented hardly a moment's worry.

On the other hand, younger brother Dean posed a seemingly insurmountable challenge to his parents and other adults who tried to take an interest in him. His behavior and attitudes reflected the timeless dilemma appreciated by beleaguered parents everywhere: What do you do with a child whose lack of ambition is matched only by his appetite for getting into trouble?

It appeared that Dean had decided, rather than living in the shadow of his accomplished brother, to cast a rather dark and disturbing one all his own. Mike describes Dean's behavior in mathematical terms: "Take all of Brian's bad traits and multiply them by five."

His assessment was not unusual. To most who knew him, Dean Baco was the antithesis of his older brother—belligerent, incorrigible, and wholly impenetrable. He forsook soccer and swimming in favor of football, a game more agreeable with his aggressive nature and one in which he was less likely to be compared to Brian.

But Dean's sense of inferiority actually may have had more to do with perception than reality. According to his father, Dean was probably a better athlete than his older brother and not far behind mentally. Yet the same family system that upheld Brian's achievements appeared to sustain Dean's delinquency. It was implicitly understood that the younger son would remain the focal point of family life. Responding to and worrying about Dean's mischief took the better part of Barbara and Herman's time. In return, the Bacos' prodigal son delivered a perpetual pattern of academic underachievement, poor impulse control, truancy, drug experimentation, fighting, and scrapes with the law.

Barbara says that she once passed out while holding Dean in her arms as an infant. When she came to, Dean was lying on the floor beside her screaming.

"I'll go to my grave thinking I did something to him," she admits.

Barbara says his problems were already apparent by age five. While taking a test in kindergarten at the Catholic school he attended, Dean indiscriminately marked responses with no thought given to what was the right or wrong answer.

As time passed, his defiance grew—as did the family's inclination to enable him in it. One day Dean was caught shoplifting merchandise from a local store. Herman's mother, who was visiting for the weekend, dismissed it as a young boy's mischief. Frustrated with the family's denial, Barbara angrily shouted at her mother-in-law, "Can't you see he's got a problem and somebody needs to help him?" Herman's mother began to cry, which, in turn, made Herman angry. Disagreement over what to do with Dean was to become a perpetual source of alienation within the family.

But while everyone was preoccupied with the bad behavior of the younger son, Brian was leading another, less exemplary life of his own. The polished public persona masked a secret life his younger brother would have appreciated. According to a friend, this alter ego got "a real source of pleasure from putting his life at risk."

Bill Geen, who joined Brian for many nights of revelry, characterizes his friend's behavior as "reckless." Furthermore, Bill contends Brian, a virtual choirboy by day, doubled as a rebel after dark, disdaining rules and violating them with impunity whenever the opportunity arose. He compared the Brian he knew to "Butthead," the irreverent cartoon figure with the noxious sense of humor.

By his mid-teens, Brian had settled into a pattern of weekend carousing with his buddies that included drinking and occasional acts of vandalism. Herman remembers that police once apprehended Brian for shoplifting at a mall store. None of this behavior was especially remarkable by the standards of adolescent mischief making. Nor is there anything extraordinary in Bill Geen's observation that his friend disliked his father and his brother and that he seemed lonely.

Still, Brian's elders likely would have been surprised by his untamed and delinquent side. As Mike pointed out, the difference between the two Baco brothers was a matter of degree rather than nature. Brian may have been far more discreet than Dean, but their mutual inclination toward self-destruction bore a striking family resemblance.

Chapter 2

By the summer of 1986, Herman had relocated to Pensacola, Florida, to take a sales position with a major Gulf Coast wine and liquor distributor. With its sandy white beaches beckoning, Brian and Dean happily joined their father there. But their relocation represented a setback to the Bacos' plan to co-parent their children. Barbara remained behind and continued to build a new life as a single person in Spartanburg. She maintained contact with her sons through weekly phone conversations and periodic weekend visits.

For Brian, Florida's initial attraction soon gave way to a bad case of homesickness. He was uncomfortable living with his father, a man he never really knew. Work, as it always had, preoccupied most of Herman's time. He gave the boys lots of freedom, which they thought they wanted, but denied them what they longed for most—himself.

The shortcomings of their living arrangement only reinforced the strength of Brian's relationship with his mother. The two of them had always shared a symbiotic attachment, one that remained intact despite the distance of hundreds of miles that now separated them.

But the void Brian felt in Florida included the absence of his friends, too. At fifteen, the move to Florida, with the demands of a new school and a parade of unfamiliar faces, proved more stressful than he had anticipated. Brian wanted to go home to Spartanburg. Finally, his parents agreed that he could return home with the provision that he must first complete the school year in Pensacola and find a part-time job to supplement the family income.

That June, after school was dismissed, Barbara drove to Florida to retrieve her boys just as the sultry summer heat began its siege upon the South. Because Barbara's car did not have air conditioning, the return trip was planned for after dark, when it would be cooler. That night Barbara, her friend Jan Brown, and the boys all piled in the car and began the long trek home to South Carolina. Their conversation that night included an ominous debate over whether or not handicapped people should be mainstreamed. Barbara favored it, while both her sons argued against it.

Eventually, talk gave way to sleep. Speeding through the quiet darkness, none of the car's passengers could foresee or even imagine the unspeakable event that awaited them.

Arriving home early on Monday morning, Brian and Dean spent much of that day sleeping and lounging about their mother's home. At some point, Brian telephoned several of his buddies and made plans for the evening. Late that afternoon, Barbara drove him to Bill Geen's house, where the friends were scheduled to spend the night. With a change of clothes under his arm, Brian kissed his mother goodbye and bounded up the driveway to Bill's house.

That evening Bill and Brian rendezvoused with their buddies, Paul Choberka, Jeff Dunham, and Rhys Gaillard. Together the boys drove to a grocery store where they purchased eggs and, with the assistance of Paul's older sister, six packs of beer. Liberated by summer vacation, the five celebrants set out in the car, alternately swigging beer and egging houses. They were young. They were free. They were also subject to a potentially dangerous sense of their own invincibility.

With their courage growing with every empty beer bottle collecting at their feet, the boys headed for an abandoned rock quarry, a popular late night destination for the teens of that community. Years of mining had carved out a cavernous pit, where, over time, water had pooled to form a pond. Standing at the rim on one side of the quarry, the water is no more than twenty feet away. But on the opposite side, where the group of friends was drawn that night, the drop is a perilous fifty feet or more. It is precisely the kind of destination parents most fear and adolescent boys, with their misguided sense of machismo, are most likely to seek out.

Bill and Brian, rivals as well as friends, often engaged in wrestling matches of such ferocity that their play threatened to erupt into fistfights. On that night, the two boys were drawn to the quarry ledge by the same excess of testosterone that drove them into such a frenzied state while wrestling.

"Geen, you don't have the balls to jump in," said Brian. "You're such a pussy."

"Oh, yeah. Well, watch this," replied Bill as he launched himself from the precipice.

Brian followed him into the water below. The other boys, more cautious or maybe with less to prove, could only stand by sheepishly and watch as the two of them, like junior Eval Knievals, matched each other plunge for fearless plunge. It might have been no more than an exhilarating start to summer vacation. But, unfortunately, the night did not end there.

If it had, Barbara's memories of the earlier part of that evening would have long been forgotten. But today, they replay over and over in her mind: Brian climbing out of the car. His goodbye kiss to her. His lean, young body running up the drive to Bill's house. It was to be the very last time she would ever see her beloved son upright.

Chapter 3

Tucked away on a piece of property in the pleasant, middle-class neighborhood that bears the idyllic name of Camelot, the Lantern Ridge Swim and Racquet Club's swimming pool sits some distance from the street and is shielded on its backside by woods. Isolated as it is and defended only by an unintimidating barbed-wire fence, the pool proved to be an irresistible attraction for the car full of young thrill seekers that night. The five boys all easily scaled the fence. Once inside, they joined in some general horseplay that included hurling lounge furniture into the pool.

By this time, it was early morning. Jeff, Rhys, and Paul crawled wearily out of the water, their energy spent, and retraced their steps back to the car. But for Bill and Brian a final challenge remained, one less intimidating but no less perilous than the leap from the rock quarry ledge.

The pool, laid out in the shape of an inverted L, has a shallow 25-meter-long vertical section used exclusively for swimming and a smaller but much deeper section reserved for diving. Flanking the swimming area on either side are metal posts approximately six feet tall bolted into the cement deck. Affixed to the top of each is a seat that serves as a lifeguard station.

Having climbed to the top of this platform, Bill decided to attempt a dive into the precariously shallow water below. To avoid hitting his head on the bottom of the pool, he had to enter the water almost horizontally. Bill successfully completed the dive, issuing an unspoken invitation for his rival to match him.

Brian immediately accepted the challenge, climbed the lifeguard stand and executed an identical dive. Then, Bill returned and completed a second dive.

While he was still submerged beneath the water, Brian mounted the lifeguard stand for his second attempt. Only this time, as he thrust himself forward, his foot slipped, sending his body sprawling toward the water below. Unable to control his descent, he pierced the water at much too steep an angle, striking his head against the concrete floor of the pool with a sickening, dull thud.

When Bill resurfaced, Brian was nowhere to be found. Assuming rightly that his buddy had followed him into the water, he waited for him to reappear. But as the seconds passed, Bill's concern grew. Either Brian was playing one of his sick pranks or something had gone terribly wrong.

Looking back over his shoulder, he saw a large, dark stain spreading ominously like an oil spill across the surface of the water, obstructing his ability to see below. With his heart pounding, Bill waded into the stain and began a frantic search of the area using his feet as probes. Soon, his foot struck something solid resting at the bottom of the pool. Drawing a deep breath into his lungs, he dove in and retrieved Brian's body. As they broke the surface of the water, he was relieved by the sound of Brian gasping for air.

Years later, Brian could still recall with perfect clarity the critical moments following the accident. Despite the fact the impact with the concrete had opened a large gash in his scalp, he never lost consciousness. The ninety seconds or so prior to his rescue took on a surreal quality, suspending time and giving him an acute awareness of his predicament.

Resting helplessly on the floor of the pool, Brian realized the air escaping his lungs represented his final link with this world. As he would later describe, he knew he was about to die, and yet, strangely, he had never felt more fully alive. Nor had his thought processes ever seemed clearer.

"Fuck. I can't move my arms and legs," he would later recall. "I bet I've hurt my spine. I don't want to be a damn vegetable. Might as well end it here."

✳ ✳ ✳ ✳ ✳ ✳ ✳ ✳

The doorbell rang at the Baco residence on White Oak Street around 2:00 a.m. on Tuesday morning. Awakened from her sleep and stumbling toward the door, Barbara had no idea what to expect.

"Who's there?" she asked cautiously.

"It's the Spartanburg police, ma'am," replied the officer standing at the door, obviously uneasy with the role that had been assigned to him.

"Ma'am, excuse me for waking you up," he said.

"That's okay," said Barbara, her sense of dread growing. "What's wrong?"

"Are you Mrs. Baco?"

"Yes. What happened?"

"Do you have a son named Brian?"

"I do. Oh, my God, what is it?"

"I'm sorry to tell you that your son has been in an accident."

The officer volunteered no information about the nature of the accident or the severity of Brian's injuries. Sensing her need for reassurance, Rhys Gaillard, who had accompanied the officer to the Bacos' home, stepped forward from the shadows to report Brian was still alive. His words, however, offered little consolation.

"I lost it," Barbara says, recalling the bad news. She broke down, her fear expressing itself in inconsolable waves of weeping. Wanting to be helpful, the officer offered her a ride to the hospital in his police cruiser.

Speeding through the night clutching the officer's arm with a half-awake Dean in tow, she tried to prepare herself for what awaited her. She could not know it at the time, but the short ride to the hospital was to be but the first leg of a life-changing odyssey.

In the emergency room of the Spartanburg General Hospital,

Barbara and Dean were escorted to the family room.

Immediately alarmed, Barbara exclaimed, "This is where they take you to tell you someone has died."

Soon after, the two of them were joined in the family room by friend Jan Brown and the chaplain on duty that night. The chaplain had no additional information to supply but reassured Barbara a doctor would be in soon to speak with her.

The EMTs who transported Brian to the emergency reported a large laceration on the top of his head and a disturbing knot on the back of his neck. Brian complained of pain in his neck and difficulty breathing. Both the technicians and the emergency room nurse who attended him described him as belligerent and uncooperative, adjectives that perhaps had never been used before in the same breath with his name.

After making a preliminary assessment that the patient's condition was stable, Dr. McGuinn, the emergency room physician, called Calvert McCorkle, a local neurosurgeon, for a consultation. McCorkle arrived at the emergency room at around 3:30 a.m. and immediately began an examination of Brian's neurological injuries. The notes he dictated that night read:

> He [Brian] was brought to the ER where lateral cervical spine x ray [sic] was taken and it showed fracture dislocation of C-5,6. . . He has a large stellate laceration at the crown of his head anteriorly of the forehead. A stellate laceration approximately 4 x 4 x 4 inches. Cranial nerves are intact. . .On motor examination, the patient is able to shrug his shoulders, and has good biceps function bilaterally. Also there is some rotation of the forearm on the left whenever he tries to flex his left arm. There are no triceps and no hand motion, and there is no movement down. The patient has a sensory level of approximately C6. He also has a priapism. There are no reflexes below the biceps. . .IMPRESSION: 1. Quadraplegia [sic], secondary to

C5, 6 fracture dislocation.

In lay terms, Brian had sustained a large, star-shaped wound on the front of his head, though there was no evidence of brain damage. More importantly, he had broken his neck between the fifth and sixth vertebrae. The dislocation of the bone had damaged the spinal cord, rendering Brian a quadriplegic, meaning he had at least partial paralysis of all four extremities.

At the time of his hospital admission on June 10, 1986, neurological transmissions were interrupted on Brian's spinal cord at the fifth cervical vertebra. Patients with this level of injury ordinarily retain some use of their arms (but not hands) and the ability to breathe on their own.

A basic rule of neurology is that the higher on the spine an injury occurs, the less physiological function a patient can expect to retain. Although the actual distance between an injury at the fifth vertebra and one located higher on the spine at the second or third vertebra is relatively small, the difference in functional quality can be quite profound. Patients with C-5 injuries can ordinarily perform a number of basic tasks necessary to their survival, from feeding themselves to holding down a job. While seriously impaired, C-5 level patients are likely to lead lives of at least partial independence.

On the other hand, those patients injured between the second and third vertebrae are destined to suffer much loss of personal autonomy. Unable to breathe on their own, they must rely on a life support system for their survival.

At 3:45 a.m., Dr. McCorkle arrived to consult with the family. Sitting across from Barbara, he explained Brian's injuries as consistent with a C-5 level spinal cord injury. Brian was breathing on his own, and according to medical records and other eyewitness accounts, was able to raise his arms. (By virtue of one of the idiosyncrasies of neurological impairment, he could not lower his arms after raising them.) There was no evidence of function in his lower arms or hands, although two visitors later reported feeling his hand contract when they grasped it.

At the moment of impact, Brian's body was instantly bisected by an invisible, horizontal line that divided him into distinct northern and southern poles. From two inches above his nipples, he retained mostly normal movement and sensation. But below that line, he was paralyzed.

McCorkle produced an X-ray from beneath his arm and, using his index finger as a pointer, traced the line of the fracture between the fifth and sixth cervical vertebrae. Barbara nodded blankly. The doctor also demonstrated for her benefit the range of motions he had observed in the patient during the examination.

While unwilling to say the paralysis was permanent, he cautioned her that it usually is. Then he sought and obtained written permission from Barbara to perform a surgical procedure to realign the broken bones. Having obtained her signature, McCorkle excused himself and hurried away.

Upon hearing the news, Barbara grew pale and began to hyperventilate. The chaplain grasped one of her hands to steady her as a nurse took the other.

"Mrs. Baco, you need to calm yourself down," said the nurse. "You've got to stay calm for Brian. He's going to need your help. You can't help him if you're getting this upset."

Her admonishment had the desired affect. With the contrition of a scolded schoolgirl, Barbara yielded to the authority of the medical staff. She breathed deeply, trying to regain her composure.

But the doctor's diagnosis of "paralysis" lingered, rattling around in her head in all its cruel incomprehensibility.

Chapter 4

Around 4:00 a.m., Barbara and Dean were finally permitted to visit Brian in the examination area of the emergency room. Self-conscious about his predicament, Brian had initially declined to see his family.

When he finally agreed to a visit, it was to be short-lived. His feelings of humiliation were compounded by the physical pain and nausea of his injury. In addition, the accident was just too fresh for words. In their shared state of shock, nothing very dramatic passed between them, nor had to. For that moment, disbelief reduced both mother and son to silence.

However, the visit did fulfill one important purpose. Seeing, touching, and talking to Brian reassured Barbara he was still alive and coherent. And her presence reassured Brian that the most irreplaceable person in his life had not abandoned him. They were two frightened people faced with an uncertain future, and it was enough for that moment to exchange token words and comforting glances.

Barbara and Dean were ushered out of the examination area and shuffled compliantly back to the family room, where Jan was anxious to know of his condition.

"How's he doing?" she asked, rubbing her friend's back.

"Well, he's paralyzed. But he's talking, and he can still move his arms some," she said. "If he can use his arms, maybe he can still have a decent life."

While the words were directed at her friend, they were clearly intended for Barbara's own benefit, as if by uttering them she could actually make them come true.

The chaplain, who was posted nearby, urged Barbara to call Herman to notify him of Brian's accident. She admits to resenting his intrusion to this day. As she sees it, there was nothing Herman could do in the middle of the night hundreds of miles away. Why deny the man one last good night of sleep before immersing him in this misery?

But the chaplain was insistent. Herman, as Brian's father, was entitled to know immediately. Barbara eventually relented, and Herman was awakened by what he describes now as "the proverbial phone call from hell." His ex-wife's words stung despite his sleepy stupor: "Brian is in the hospital. He is paralyzed."

With his instincts taking over, Herman returned the phone to its cradle, dressed quickly, and sped off into the night. The nonstop dash to Spartanburg was powered by pure adrenaline. In his own enigmatic way, the reaction was consistent with his image of himself as a devoted father. He might be emotionally distant and even physically absent much of the time, owing to his obsession with work, but in his mind, there was no confusion or contradiction. His love for his boys was unquestionable. Earning a living, coaching their soccer teams, and coming home each night were evidence of his devotion.

Practically speaking, there was little Herman could do in the crisis. But as Brian's father, practicality was no consideration at all in his 700-mile dash to Spartanburg in the middle of the night. His child was in trouble, and he had to go to him.

Meanwhile, Dr. McCorkle ordered the staff to transfer Brian to a Stryker bed frame. The Stryker bed could be manually rotated a full 360 degrees within its frame, making it especially useful for patients unable to shift and redistribute their body weight.

Now obsolete, this ingenious piece of hospital equipment was designed to relieve pressure on an immobilized patient's skin, reducing the risk of developing painful and debilitating bedsores. At prescribed intervals over the course of a 24-hour period, a patient confined to a Stryker frame could be rotated from a right side up position to upside down. Padded bars across the forehead, chin and along the length of the body secured the patient while suspended in the inverted position. In the days to come, Brian's body would revolve on the axis of his Stryker frame, leaving him alternately staring at the floor and ceiling.

Another important task of those early post-accident days spent in the NICU was to stabilize the injured area to prevent further damage to Brian's severely traumatized spinal tissue. In medical terminology, a misalignment of bone caused by a fracture is called a subluxation.

Just as a doctor must reset a broken arm to promote proper healing, so McCorkle was preparing to realign the broken bone in Brian's neck. The procedure sometimes used with such injuries calls for screwing twin metal braces called Gardner-Wells tongs directly into the skull. By anchoring the tongs with weights and gradually increasing the tension in five to ten pound increments, the cervical bone is pulled back into realignment, reducing the risk the fractured bone will do even greater damage to the suddenly exposed spinal cord.

Beginning with a 25-pound base, McCorkle had the tension on Brian's traction increased incrementally by a total of 72 pounds of pressure in just a matter of minutes. The procedure proved to be temporarily successful. A radiologist's report comparing X-rays taken at the time of his arrival with those following the application of the Gardner-Wells tongs confirmed there had been a measurable reduction in the subluxation.

In the hours following the accident, it must have seemed incomprehensible that Brian, this enthusiastic and precocious teenager, was facing life with a permanent disability. At almost sixteen years of age, the Bacos' elder son was progressing happily toward a life of greater autonomy. Within a month he would qualify for a South Carolina driver's license, a venerable cultural symbol of adult privilege and freedom. A couple of years later, upon successful completion of his high school education, he expected to enroll in college to study for his life's work. For his parents and others who cherished him, there was a contentment in watching Brian mature, a satisfaction that comes from the knowledge a young person's life is charting a predictable and timeless trajectory. But with one foolish slip, destiny made an unanticipated and irrevocable U-turn. Brian had regressed to the dependency of a child.

Chapter 5

S trapped into the Stryker frame and with the Gardner-Wells tongs bolted snugly into his skull, Brian began his descent into the bizarre world of neurological intensive care. It is a world that never sleeps— it can't afford to. Tubes were joined to Brian's body, and monitors, beeping and glowing, kept their watch through the night like electronic shepherds. Rest—what there was of it—came in fits. Receiving periodic injections of codeine for pain, Brian was lost for days in a semi-conscious haze.

Thanks to the Stryker frame, he would wake up one hour with the ceiling above him and hours later find himself staring at the floor tiles below. A nurse roused him to check his vital signs, then minutes later, or so it seemed, a different nurse from a different shift would be standing over him. There were visits from people unknown to him who appeared unannounced to stare, poke, prod, and ask a litany of questions, all of which he had answered a dozen times before.

In that dreamlike state, life resembled a scene from Alice's Wonderland. Strangers were everywhere, while his parents, the two people he most longed to see, were largely unavailable to him. The searing pain radiating from his neck clashed with the absence of any sensation over the lower two-thirds of his body. Strapped in, bolted down, and hooked up, it was all stranger than the science fiction he adored.

McCorkle and his partner, Dr. Robert Flandry, made regular

morning and evening rounds to monitor their patient's condition. Round-the-clock care was provided in shifts by nurses assigned to the neuro unit.

This medical team, experienced in the special care of severe spinal cord injuries, appreciated the gravity of the situation. Many series of X-rays were taken and carefully examined during Brian's eight-day ordeal there to assure the broken neck bone did not slip out of its fragile realignment. If it shifted just a millimeter or two, the fractured bone could pinch down on the cord, causing further damage to the vulnerable spinal tissue. The equivalent of thirty-nine thousandths of an inch, a millimeter hardly registers as a blip on the metric scale. And yet the spinal cord is an extraordinarily delicate tissue. Encased as it is within the narrow spinal column, the margin for error in such cases can be infinitesimally small. A seemingly minor shift of bone could mean a major difference in the outcome for a patient.

The Baco family huddled tensely with friends in the waiting room. They hung on to the trickle of information from infrequent encounters with Brian's doctors.

Some physicians manage to respond to their patients and the families with generosity and graciousness, but sadly, many do not. They understand their responsibility to treat the patient, while ignoring the equally critical role of attending to family members who are scared silly. This inattention is sometimes attributed to "compassion fatigue" or busy schedules, but whatever the reason, it compounds the suffering of families and reinforces doctors' reputations as mere body mechanics.

Barbara was displeased with the unavailability of the neurosurgeons treating her son in those critical days following his accident: "I remember being very upset with him [one of McCorkle's partners] because, you know, he wasn't volunteering anything. I didn't know if Brian was on the verge of death. I didn't get that from any of them. I saw all three of them, and they certainly would not volunteer anything to me. I didn't know if Brian was dying or what. Any nobody would tell me anything."

As if compensating for the disheartening state of doctor/patient relations, registered nurses routinely step in to fill the compassion void. As the primary caregivers to their patients, they are often pressed into double duty as intermediaries, relaying messages between doctors and patients' families. Much of what loved ones will learn about a patient's condition, as well as medical information in general, they will get from nurses. Balancing the demands of long, stressful shifts in often under-staffed units with a kind regard for those they serve, the nursing profession is proof that technical competence and compassion are not necessarily mutually exclusive. While the title M.D. confers prestige, it may be the nurses who are the medical system's most indispensable resource. Yet the fact that many communities today face a critical shortage of registered nurses may very well speak to a general lack of respect for the profession.

The birth of the NICU at Spartanburg General Hospital in 1972 coincided with the arrival of Dr. Darwin Keller. The young neurosurgeon, fresh out of his residency in Charleston, exactly doubled the number of neurosurgeons practicing in Spartanburg. He not only referred his patients to the fledgling unit but also served as a technical consultant, teaching his specialty to the group of nurses assembled to staff it. He was joined by a former ICU nurse who was appointed to supervise the unit. Together, they formed a remarkably "green" critical care team. As nurse Kathy Johnson now admits, the staff cut their neurological teeth by "a little trial and error." It was hardly the standard for treating patients with life-threatening neurological conditions, but by the standards of a sleepy mill town, this new critical care unit represented measurable progress in the way local medicine was practiced.

A pleasant, middle-aged woman with a soft Southern drawl, one senses a rock solid stability in Kathy's demeanor. She possesses what is rare in today's restless world, a sense of history in one community. Hers is a value system firmly rooted in a keen sense of duty: that a person's word makes a written contract unnecessary. Over the last thirty years, the Spartanburg hospital system has undergone radical transformations, including a name change. Yet the one thing that has remained constant throughout is the Kathy Johnsons of its staff, reliably punching the clock each workday.

When Kathy arrived for work the morning after Brian was

admitted, she was assigned to his case. Examining his chart, she noted the diagnosis of a broken neck. She also observed that the patient shrugged his shoulders and that he had feeling from the chest up. Throughout that first day, she was preoccupied with charting his vital statistics, adjusting the amount of weight holding him in traction, and administering doses of codeine for pain as prescribed by Dr. McCorkle. In between these duties, she kept the family apprised of Brian's condition.

It was to be a difficult and perplexing case for her and others who were involved. For in Brian Baco, they were about to witness the realization of one of neurology's worst fears.

Chapter 6

At 7:30 on the morning of Brian's admission to the hospital, Dr. McCorkle had scribbled a note to himself on the patient's chart: "will plan surgery." After the formal admission process, he returned to Barbara's side to discuss two possible treatment options: either confine Brian to traction for six weeks and hope the bone would heal naturally, or perform an operation called a fusion.

The surgery called for transplanting two small bone grafts from the hip to the site of the injury and wiring them in place in the fashion of a splint. The expectation was that in time the transplanted bone would grow together, or fuse, with the fractured vertebra in a solid, reinforced mass.

The alternate strategy of traction, while non-invasive, offered no guarantee of success. In the hours after Brian was first fitted with the Gardner-Wells tongs, traction had succeeded in reducing the misalignment of the broken bone. Whether the fix would hold and become permanent could not be guaranteed. If, after six weeks in traction the bone failed to mend properly, Brian would still face surgery.

In addition, the degree of immobilization required by traction made him susceptible to developing bedsores. A nemesis of every long-term bedridden patient, once these hideous ulcerations form at pressure points along the surface of the body they are very difficult to heal.

Barbara gave her consent to the surgery that first morning. Her decision was predicated, she says, upon one critical factor: the unknown impact six weeks of traction might have on her son's mental state. As she explained it in a deposition almost two years later, ". . . by this time also, the hospital social worker had come up and told me what good news that Dr. McCorkle was going to send Brian to Shepherd Spinal Center in Atlanta and what a wonderful place that was and how they worked with patients and all that. So there was no reason to dream of Brian lying in bed in traction for six weeks when he could be at the hospital receiving therapy." She hoped the change of venue, coupled with the promise of rehabilitation, would gird her son with some much-needed optimism that his condition was improving.

Barbara cannot remember Dr. McCorkle expressing a treatment preference at the time. Apparently, he laid out the pair of options rather dispassionately and left the decision to her. Still, she inferred from their conversation that he was "leaning toward" surgery, which was later confirmed by the note he had earlier jotted to himself on the patient's chart. It seems plausible she was intuiting a surgeon's bias for the more aggressive approach to treat the injury.

After Herman arrived at the hospital early the afternoon of June 10, McCorkle reviewed the two treatment options with both parents. Speaking candidly with the Bacos, he told them that the proposed surgery would only stabilize the broken bone. It could not correct the paralysis nor would it restore Brian to his pre-injured state. He also explained possible complications of surgery, noting that there was a risk the operation might further damage spinal tissue that was already badly bruised and swollen. The dilemma confronting Brian's parents was the absence of a clear course to take on a subject about which they, as lay people, were painfully uninformed. As they understood it, six weeks in traction offered no promises, but then neither did the surgery.

All that remained was for Herman to give his consent. When he raised no objection, McCorkle reserved an operating room for June 12. On the morning of the twelfth, Kathy Johnson began to prep Brian for surgery, and around 1:30, Brian was wheeled into the surgical suite. McCorkle was joined in the operating room that day by orthopedic surgeon Dr. Donald McClure for what was to be a surgical procedure in two distinct movements.

The opening movement belonged to McClure, who was responsible for obtaining two bone grafts from Brian's hip. After the grafts of bone, each approximately one inch wide by four inches long, were obtained and the incision closed, McCorkle set to work on fusing them in place. For this part of the procedure, Brian remained on the Stryker frame facing the floor.

Once X-rays were taken to measure the existing subluxation and proper alignment at the site of the fracture, the surgeon began the tedious process of exposing the damaged bone. The spinal column is encased in layers of muscle, ligaments, and other sinewy, connective tissue that had to be retracted to prepare the surface of vertebrae four through seven to receive the graft. McCorkle then used a special drill to "burr up" the finish on the freshly exposed bones. Next, he delicately guided a curved needle threaded with 20 and 28-gauge wire around each vertebra, careful not to disturb the damaged tissue. The bone struts taken from the hip were affixed on either side of the fracture, and the wires tightened to secure them in place.

The whole procedure required less than three hours to complete. By the time Brian was returned to the NICU at 5:45 p.m., a hospital bed had been substituted for the Stryker frame. McCorkle also replaced the Gardner-Wells tongs with a somi brace, which is fitted around the chest and shoulders and includes a metal bar that connects the chin to the chest piece to immobilize the neck while simultaneously supporting the weight of the head. For most of the remainder of that evening, Brian drifted in and out of consciousness. As late as 10:00 p.m., the nurse on duty was still observing weak movements in his arms.

But by 4:00 the next morning, Brian began complaining of difficulty breathing. Feeling anxious, he appealed to the nurse to remain at his side. When the breathing problems persisted, he panicked, demanding to know what was wrong. The nurse responded by fitting him with an oxygen mask. But fifteen minutes later, she observed that his mouth was open and that he was gasping for air like a sprinter who has just crossed the finish line. Realizing that her patient's condition was deteriorating, she quickly notified Dr. Flandry, who was on call that night.

Flandry ordered blood gases to be analyzed and asked that Dr. Joe T. Wills, the surgical resident on call, be paged to examine the patient. The respiratory therapist on duty was also called and produced an ambu bag to begin manually pumping oxygen into Brian's depleted lungs. Unresponsive to the intervention and barely conscious, Brian's condition was growing more critical by the minute.

Dr. Wills instructed the nurse to administer a dose of Narcan. Since his admission, Brian had been receiving regular injections of codeine for the pain in his neck. Strong narcotics, such as codeine, are known to produce side effects that can include suppressed respiration. If Brian's breathing problems were caused by his medication, Narcan would counteract its effect and restore normal respiratory patterns.

When there was no improvement, Wills ordered a second dose of Narcan, followed by a third and fourth. Somewhere between the last two injections Brian became more alert and his breathing patterns more regular. It was 5:20 in the morning by the time the ambu bag could be safely withdrawn. The crisis had been averted—temporarily.

Only a few hours later, however, Kathy Johnson found her young patient in distress once more. Analysis of a blood sample confirmed what the staff suspected: the oxygen level being assimilated by Brian's lungs was insufficient to sustain his life.

Dr. Flandry instructed Kathy to request a consultation with Charles Fogarty, a local pulmonary specialist. Fogarty, who was unavailable at the time, advised her instead to contact a nurse anesthetist to perform an intubation procedure. An oxygen mask is often inadequate for a patient with a critical respiratory problem because some air tends to escape from beneath the mask. The anesthetist inserted a plastic tube into Brian's nose, threaded it through the nasal cavity, and brought it to rest at the entrance of the tracheal passage, assuring that 100 percent of the oxygen supply reached his lungs.

A chest X-ray confirmed proper placement of the tube. The respiratory therapist then tested Brian's vital capacity, which measured the volume of air he was able to inhale into his lungs. Anything less than 500 cubic centimeters is generally considered insufficient to sustain life. At the time of the test, Brian's vital capacity measured only 300 ccs.

Thirty minutes later, without any sign of improvement, Brian was placed on a mechanical respirator.

When the doctor finally made his way to the waiting room to consult with Barbara, it was 9:00 a.m. Five full hours had elapsed since the first sign of the crisis. She had left her son the night before in stable condition, only to return that next morning to be greeted by the news he had been placed on life support.

Barbara was furious that the staff had failed to call and report that her son was in distress. The nurse's notes from that night clearly document the panic she observed in his face. Yet this fifteen-year-old boy was allowed to face a life-threatening situation without his parents being made aware of the crisis.

Brian was essentially suffocating that night, the fear he felt compounded by a strangely unresponsive body. He could not raise his hands to his throat to signal distress nor could he run for help. The nurse by his side became his lifeline. The predicament was as cruel for its irony as for the panic it evoked in him. Oxygen, an essential element of life, was all about him, yet his diaphragm and brain were suddenly unable to coordinate the means to suck it into his lungs. What the day before had been effortless and involuntary was now incomprehensibly hard. The fight for survival that night was to leave an indelible impression upon Brian's newly vulnerable psyche.

The ordeal dragged on for several more torturous days. Brian would complain of shortness of breath. The nurse on duty responded by paging either Fogarty or Flandry. The doctor ordered the respirator setting adjusted to increase the volume of oxygen being forced into his lungs. For a short time, the increased flow of oxygen satisfied his body's needs, allowing Brian to rest comfortably. But invariably, sometimes only a matter of minutes later, the shortness of breath returned, triggering the same sequence of events all over again. With each upward adjustment of the dial on the respirator, his dependence on the life support system grew less and less negotiable.

"He was going downhill," recalls Kathy Johnson. She and the other nurses went back and forth to the waiting room to relay the disheartening news to the family. "Man," she says, "that was a stressful day, I can tell you."

The medical staff was preoccupied during that time with obtaining two crucial pieces of information about their patient's condition: the cause of his respiratory distress as well as the extent of it.

The hope, of course, was that the diminished capacity of his respiratory system was temporary and that normal function would soon return. Periodically, Brian was removed from the respirator to measure his breathing capacity. With each test, though, his heart rate fell to thirty beats per minute and his vital capacity topped out at a dismal 50 ccs.

After three days of experimentation, there was no denying the dismal truth. The neurological signals between Brian's brain and his diaphragm were failing. Without the necessary expansion and contraction of the muscles that encased his lungs, self-sufficient breathing was impossible. By the time the respiratory testing was abandoned, the medical staff had grudgingly arrived at the grim conclusion that their patient's paralysis had ascended.

It would go down in the medical literature as one of those freakish aberrations where the loss of neurological function progressed above the level of the original injury. The shoulder shrugs that grew progressively weaker were a visible sign of Brian's failing respiratory function. By the day of his discharge on June 18, the shrugs, like the ability to breathe on his own, had disappeared entirely.

Gone for good were all voluntary muscle control and sensation below the neck. And with their passing, the expectations for the quality of his life were revised regrettably downward. He was reclassified as a complete C2-3 quadriplegic.

From that time forward, Brian Baco would be bound permanently to a respirator. Even momentary separation from this artificial life support system would mean certain death by suffocation.

Chapter 7

Along with his deteriorating physical condition, Brian's mental state was slumping badly. He refused invitations to listen to music or to watch television, and he shunned visitors except for his parents. While sleep offered a temporary reprieve, he invariably wakened to the nightmare that never went away—one that would ultimately prove invulnerable to either positive thinking or prayer. With the growing awareness that his condition was irreversible, Brian now wept openly and often, and slumped into a clinical depression virtually inseparable from misery of this magnitude.

However, on the afternoon of June 17, just a day before his scheduled discharge from the hospital, a social worker visited Brian to inform him of his transfer by air ambulance the following day to the Shepherd Spinal Center in Atlanta.

A broad smile, the first anyone had seen in more than a week, warmed his gloomy countenance. Not even the events of the previous seven days could dull his enthusiasm over the rare opportunity to fly in an airplane.

And just as Barbara had hoped, the news of the change of venue seemed to give him a moral boost. Brian spoke by phone with the nurse who would be responsible for his care at Shepherd. During their conversation, he expressed a surprising eagerness to begin his rehabilitation.

With his spirits temporarily lifted, he agreed at last to receive visitors, a decision that brought a parade of friends and well-wishers to his bedside. The hospital room took on the appearance of a pep rally as one by one his teammates, classmates, teachers, neighbors, and friends stepped forward to offer encouragement. Brian's high school soccer coach presented him with a warm-up suit for the trip to Atlanta. A spirit of goodwill descended upon Brian that day and broke through his despair. Bolstered by the encouragement of family and friends, he appeared to be the cheerful Brian of old.

The scene that afternoon defied the devastation Brian felt inside. Visitors could not see beneath his courteous smile that even then, Brian Baco was undergoing a transformation of the most radical kind. Gone for good was the carefree optimism of the past. The colossal challenge of trying to inhabit a largely uninhabitable body had seen to that.

The next day the air ambulance arrived for the 160-mile flight from Spartanburg to Atlanta. Located on Peachtree Road, downtown Atlanta's most prominent traffic artery, the Shepherd Spinal Center was founded in 1975 as a result of a tragic accident that visited the family of Alana and Harold Shepherd.

Their son, James, suffered a spinal cord injury in a freakish body surfing accident. Unable to locate a rehabilitation facility anywhere in the South to treat spinal injuries, the Shepherds traveled as far as Colorado seeking appropriate care for their son. Happily, James' condition improved in time, and he was eventually able to walk again with the aid of crutches. But the family's experience convinced them of the need to establish a facility in the Southeast that would specialize in the care and treatment of patients with spinal cord injuries.

The Shepherd family, owners of a road construction company, was guided in the beginning only by a vision of what could be. With no prior knowledge of either medicine or fundraising, they set out in all their naiveté to build a state-of-the-art facility in Atlanta. They were, of course, rudely greeted by skeptics in the medical establishment who questioned the feasibility of their vision.

"I guess if a family in the medical community told me they were going into the road building business, I would look at them funny, too," admits Harold Shepherd in some of the organization's promotional material.

In the end, however, the family's determination prevailed. With the help of Dr. David Apple, an orthopedist they managed to lure away from private practice to serve as their first medical director, Shepherd Spinal Center opened modestly in an existing hospital wing with six beds and a waiting list of patients. Under Apple's direction, it eventually grew into one of the largest, most respected spinal cord injury centers in the country, offering an impressive array of innovative programs and services.

A unique feature of Shepherd Center is its uninterrupted relationship with the founders. Members of the Shepherd family continue to serve on its board of directors and work with patients and their families. Instead of the passing interest of a detached benefactor who merely writes a check, theirs is the empathy of survivors, who fully appreciate the impact severe spinal cord injuries have upon patients and their families.

Yet, in some respects, it is difficult for a thoughtful observer to separate the Shepherds' personal passion for this cause from the perpetual burden to raise money necessary to fund research and development by presenting its work in the best possible light. Shepherd's quarterly publication, *Spinal Column,* is chockfull of smiling glossies and tightly worded tributes to former patients who have triumphed over their disabilities. This, coupled with tours of the facility led by a perky, young guide, indicate the public relations machine is hard at work spinning tales of inspiration to warm the hearts and loosen the pocketbooks of prospective donors. The subtitle of a feature on a former patient, ". . .life is five percent what happens to you, and 95 percent how you handle it," displays a positive thinking flair that would make Norman Vincent Peale beam.

Yet the institution is still very much a work in progress. To be sure, Shepherd has been at the forefront of some astonishing developments in the treatment of spinal cord injuries. But it is also apparent that the road ahead is long and arduous, with every single advancement raising as many questions as it resolves. Under highly stressful circumstances, rehabilitation becomes a riddle to solve that leaves staff to sort through a tangle of competing needs and interests.

Unfortunately, in prioritizing a treatment plan, the limitations of time and resources mean some important issues of a patient's life may have to go unaddressed. Each unresolved issue represents a potential disruption capable of sabotaging that individual's adjustment to disability.

When Brian was admitted to Shepherd in 1986, the rehabilitation process moved at a relatively leisurely pace measured in months. But in today's rapid-fire world of managed care, treatment tends to get meted out in stingy 28-day portions. One of the more insidious practices of our current system of standardization is the rush to discharge.

Dr. William Bockenek, director of the Spinal Cord Injury Program at the Charlotte Institute of Rehabilitation, refers to "critical pathways" (a business term for maximizing efficiency and minimizing costs) that permeate the present practice of medicine. But the truth, he says, is that patients, unlike manufactured goods, do not always respond to prescribed treatments in predictable ways or in a pre-determined time frame.

And yet in the current climate, managed care dictates that in the breathtakingly brief span of four weeks, victims of catastrophic neurological injuries and diseases must be equipped to re-enter the world of the unimpaired. This expectation heightens the likelihood that patients will be discharged prematurely into families that may very well be unprepared to receive them.

Chapter 8

Shepherd Center is distinguished from more conventional medical facilities because its patients are admitted with little to no expectation of getting well. Given the grimness of outcomes that include the loss of vital bodily functions and serious psychological distress, the traditional Western approach to healing, with its imperative for full and speedy recovery, has undergone a major overhaul at Shepherd Center.

Of necessity, convalescence has been reoriented toward the development of skills that emphasize maximizing one's capacity to accept and adjust to disability. Prominent in the Shepherd model is a "community re-entry" strategy that prepares patients to cope with a non-disabled world that is often unwilling to accommodate them. This includes public outings to desensitize them to gawking strangers and insulting comments and invasive questions that will become an everyday feature of their new lives.

Recognizing that physical disability leaves no dimension of a person's life untouched, Shepherd Center has moved toward a holistic approach to rehabilitation. Standard care today features services such as recreational therapy, psychological counseling, peer support, career planning, and vocational services. In addition to conventional types of medical services, it offers disability rights advocacy; special interest classes that include swimming; art and aerobics; sponsorship of competing basketball, rugby, track and fencing teams; skills workshops;

summer camps for children, and AA groups. And the list continues to grow each year as appreciation of the needs of disabled people deepens.

James Shepherd explains the holistic approach this way: "Our patients are here to re-enter life. Although we do map a critical path for them, we want the patient's and family's input to pick the goals and options that are important to them. That gives people control over their destiny."

And that is true to a degree. While a patient's "destiny" will be determined somewhat by the careful management of his or her life, it will also ultimately hinge upon the severity of the impairment. Not all spinal cord injuries are created equal.

Even an impairment as severe as Brian's is not the worst. No sight at Shepherd is quite so sobering as that of patients with brain stem injuries. Damage that occurs to the spinal cord at the base of the brain results in the most debilitating damage to the central nervous system. These patients walk the finest line between life and death, their stillness only occasionally interrupted by the blinking of their eyes. They are human beings, complete with personality traits, emotions, and intelligence, entombed in unresponsive bodies. Of course, most of Shepherd's patients are not this profoundly impaired, but virtually all will be asked to make accommodations to their disabilities that are bound to leave them feeling deprived and cheated.

Shepherd Center was to serve as Brian's home for the next five months of his life. After the initial excitement of the transfer subsided, he again sank into despair. Individuals who suffer losses of this magnitude are subject to erratic and dramatic mood swings. They are likely to career wildly between episodes of intense sadness and unprovoked rage. Appearing to be adjusting well one moment, they may seem crushed the next. Their capacity to cope with this keen psychic pain is likely to correspond to the size and strength of the support system at their disposal.

In this regard, Brian was distinctly disadvantaged. He suddenly found himself in a strange city where he knew no one. (Ironically, his ambition had been to attend Georgia Tech, which is also located in Atlanta.) With the immediate crisis behind them, his parents were now torn between their obligation to him and the reality that life, with its routine responsibilities, goes on. Another child (and a high-maintenance one at that) awaited them at home. There were jobs to do and bills to pay.

Barbara and Herman rendezvoused in Atlanta most weekends to be available to their son, their commutes always coming at the end of exhausting workweeks. (Barbara missed only one weekend during Brian's entire stay at Shepherd.) When there was no money for motel rooms, they slept on mats on Shepherd's gym floor. They subsisted on fast food and whatever they could rustle up in the facility's kitchen. Friends and family made occasional day trips supplemented with cards and letters expressing their support.

But no sentiment could assuage a young boy's devastation. One of Barbara's most vivid memories of Shepherd was the sight of her son lying in bed with a washcloth draped over his face. The staff tried to reassure her the phenomenon was not unusual. Besides their usefulness as tools to manipulate one's environment, hands can serve as convenient shrouds for masking human shame and/or misery from the world. But quadriplegia denies its victims even this most basic "face-saving" gesture. The washcloth then represents one of the patient's first adaptations to what his hands can no longer do for him.

As Brian later would admit to me, the shame he felt was profound. We were talking one afternoon about his predicament, when he suddenly diverted his eyes to gaze out the window.

"Dumb," he said. "Really dumb."

"What's dumb?" I asked.

"What I've done to myself."

This kid with an impressive track record for getting things right, had, for once in his life, got it wrong—terribly, terribly wrong. For those who knew his story, his disability would always be linked to that fateful night of drinking and carousing. While residents of Spartanburg would befriend him with many heartfelt gestures, always implicit in the sight of this crippled teen strapped in a wheelchair was the realization his misery was self-inflicted. Also implicated were his parents. Persons close to the family point out that discipline relaxed for the Baco sons after their parents' divorce.

Overlooked in their logic, of course, is the fact there were four other teenagers present at the scene of the accident that night. And quite certainly, there are many others from intact families who have engaged in behavior as bad or worse. Most of the time, we survive our youthful indiscretions unscathed. But Brian did not. His withered arms and legs would serve as a painful daily reminder of his lapse. And the judgment of others would be nothing as compared with the indictment he brought against himself: "Dumb. Really dumb."

Thus, teaching Brian the physical skills he would need for his survival was simple compared with addressing his emotional distress and restoring his will to live. A stack of photos from his days at Shepherd Center includes a series of shots from a Halloween costume party thrown by the staff just days before his discharge. Brian's costume consists of a cardboard box decorated to look like a television set placed over his head. Framed within the screen of the television he wears a Max Headroom mask, complete with a chiseled chin and an impressive array of pearly whites.

But one particular photo in the collection is especially haunting. It is the one in which Brian's mask has been removed from his face. The stiff, forced smile is the pose of an individual determined not to spoil the fun of others. The facial expression he wears suggests that he is fully aware of the absurdity of his situation—a catastrophic spinal cord injury set against the backdrop of party frivolity. The fake smile making his face ache is actually part of his training for life as a disabled person. It masks the truth that he doesn't want to be there. What's more, he doesn't want this life. He would like nothing better than to climb out of that abominable wheelchair and return home to his previous life of accomplishment and freedom.

Chapter 9

Barbara remained at her son's side during the first three weeks of his stay at Shepherd Spinal Center. But after exhausting all her accumulated leave at work, she was forced to return to Spartanburg to save her job. But every Friday afternoon, thereafter, she climbed into her old Celica to make the three-hour drive and take up temporary residence at Shepherd. Sleeping on mats in its gym and making use of its bathroom facilities, she seldom wandered far from Brian's side. When he turned up his nose at the bland cafeteria food served to him, she gratefully ate it before retrieving the fast food he wanted. The pattern already beginning to emerge was one that would define her life. Her suffocatingly small world was now comprised of essentially two things—her job and responsibility for Brian.

One Friday evening soon after his arrival at Shepherd, Barbara kissed Brian goodbye and shuffled her tired body off to a motel room. She had just crawled into bed when a nurse in the special care unit called to say Brian had "a little bleeder" around his tracheal tube. With no tone of urgency in the nurse's voice, Barbara thanked her and asked to be notified during the night if there was any change in his condition. It wasn't long before the phone rang again. This time the voice on the other end of the line identified himself as Dr. Turk. He reported Brian's condition had deteriorated, and he urged her to return to Shepherd as quickly as possible.

A dazed Barbara dashed through the facility's front door a few minutes later and headed straight for her son's room on the third floor. But she was intercepted en route by a nurse who redirected her to Piedmont Hospital next door where Brian had been taken for emergency treatment. Making her way breathlessly along the tunnel connecting the two facilities, her maternal alarm sounded once again just as it had the night of the accident.

In the hospital's waiting room Barbara learned that the tracheal tube carrying oxygen to Brian's lungs had eroded a hole in the innominate artery of his neck, causing a major hemorrhage. It was later discovered that he was born with an unusual bend in this artery that had gone undetected at the time of his tracheotomy.

Later, Barbara learned why the nurse had headed her off in the hallway. The ruptured artery had spewed blood all over Brian's room. His survival was itself a miracle. If Jimmy Smith, the nurse on duty that evening, had not been present in Brian's room at the time the rupture occurred, he would have soon bled to death. Smith, acting instinctively, stanched the spraying blood with his finger. Once the hemorrhage was brought under control, Shepherd personnel rushed Brian next door to Piedmont Hospital where a surgical team was prepping to repair the damaged artery.

There in the waiting room, a surgeon warned Barbara that Brian's condition was critical and that he might not survive the surgery. If he did survive, the substantial amount of blood he had lost could mean permanent brain damage. But Brian did survive, and he was returned to his room at Shepherd the next day. As the attendant wheeled him from the elevator, Barbara rushed to his side.

"Brian," she said softly, calling out his name.

He opened his eyes, smiled weakly, and mouthed the words, "Hey Mom."

She smiled back, stroking his hair. At that moment, she knew he would be okay. For the second time in less than a month, Brian's life had been spared by a well-meaning act of heroism. His ambivalence about the nurse's intervention was identical to his reaction regarding the pool rescue. Initial relief would soon give way again to gloom. While appreciative, on one hand, of Smith's expert response, Brian would ultimately return to the same thorny question as before: Exactly what were they saving him from or for?

Just as he secretly wished to have been left to drown at the bottom of the pool, he now expressed a preference for a merciful death by hemorrhaging. Not quite sixteen years old, he had already begun to formulate a personal ethic about the right to die. Death, he concluded, was superior to an existence defined by deprivation.

During his stay at Shepherd, Brian repeatedly expressed his desire to die to anyone who would listen. Gabe Volk, his longtime soccer coach and friend, recalls being startled by what he heard on one of his visits to see Brian at Shepherd.

"We're all rooting for you to get better and get out of here," said Gabe.

"I'm not going to get better," he replied. "I just want to pull the plug on that stupid machine and be done with it."

A staff physician attending the case diagnosed the death wish as symptomatic of the severe depression that usually accompanies severe spinal cord injuries and referred Brian to a psychiatrist for treatment. The family was told that depression and his bizarre behavior were all symptomatic of Brian's struggle to accept his new life.

During an unusually turbulent period early in his rehabilitation, he grew increasingly more belligerent. The uncharacteristic behavior was reinforced by his roommate at the time. Ken, also a young male, had been wounded by stray gunfire as he stood innocently in a phone booth making a call. The bullet ripped through his spinal cord, leaving him a complete quadriplegic. The incomprehensibility of this random, senseless act of violence left him understandably bitter. Ken's rage commingled with Brian's and formed a collective fury their room could barely contain. Much of it, unfortunately, was directed with particular vehemence at the Shepherd staff.

A nasty set of fangs replaced Brian's formerly polite and pleasant public demeanor. If his body had been functional, the desire to lash out might have made him dangerous. As it was, it simply made him intolerable to be around. One day, without any provocation, he spat upon a nurse. The nurse was so shaken by the contemptuous gesture she threatened to seek reassignment. Barbara dismissed the outbursts as an "ugly spell" she blamed on Ken's bad influence.

For despondent spinal cord patients, especially the males, expressions of anger may feel less threatening than expressing fear and sadness. If there was anything redeemable about Brian and Ken's insufferable behavior during that time, it was that both young men were trying, however clumsily, to come to terms with a loss of epic proportions. And if there was anything encouraging about their rage, it was as evidence that quadriplegia had not succeeded in snuffing out their will to fight back.

Chapter 10

With Brian's discharge from Shepherd approaching, the question of what would become of him preoccupied Barbara and Herman's attention. Specific plans had to be quickly formulated for his care.

At the time of his accident, no nursing home in the state of South Carolina accepted respirator-dependent patients. In fact, Barbara recalls that only two such facilities on the entire East Coast were agreeable to absorbing the labor costs associated with taking patients who require such a high level of care. Besides the inconvenience of relocating him to another community, Barbara was determined not to institutionalize her son. Her own sensitivity to abandonment was too keen to subject Brian to that.

The only other recourse available to the family was for one of the parents to assume his guardianship and supplement that with in-home nursing care. Brian was partial to his mother, and she alone was prepared to make the necessary sacrifice to provide for his daily care.

"He was mine," she explains. "And that's what you do when you have children—take care of them."

Barbara could not know the magnitude of the commitment she was about to make. The care of a high-level quadriplegic demands all the energy and resourcefulness of the parent of a newborn, and then some. For unlike a healthy child, Brian the quadriplegic was not going to grow up and leave home. He would never again walk, feed himself, or provide for his own personal hygiene. Nor was he likely to ever gain financial independence. The exceptional degree of impairment, coupled with the complications of their care, make respirator-dependent quadriplegics among the least employable of the disabled population. What Barbara faced was a lifetime obligation. Yet no one was prepared to predict whether that lifetime was hers or his.

At the time of his discharge, Shepherd Spinal Center had just celebrated its first decade of existence. The science of rehabilitation was still in its infancy, making the Baco family pioneers of a sort. The staff provided counseling to equip Barbara as best they could for the enormous task ahead, but their best collective wisdom was destined to wilt in the white heat of actual life experience.

Barbara describes how the extent of Brian's physical therapy consisted of "teaching him to sit up." Her comment, uttered partially in jest, was hardly facetious.

A quadriplegic patient is especially vulnerable to bedsores and respiratory ailments. The risk of each increases proportionately to the amount of time the patient remains bed-bound. It is imperative in the rehabilitation process to move these patients into an inclined position as quickly as possible. Many are only able to sit at a 45-degree angle at first because of a combination of fatigue and anxiety about getting an insufficient supply of air. But in this semi-inclined position they cannot easily interact with others and perform the skills necessary to operate their wheelchairs. Because the ability to sit upright improves the patient's overall quality of life, the staff considers it critical to help them develop the endurance to do so. Still, it sometimes takes months before the patient feels comfortable in this position.

One of the crucial factors in Shepherd's program is the amount of attention paid to the family members who will serve as caregivers. After training Brian to speak with the aid of a respirator and to operate his sip and puff wheelchair, it was Barbara who got the real education in survival skills. The staff groomed her for the assortment of roles she would play: nurse, dietitian, physical therapist, respiratory therapist, social worker, hygienist, psychologist, chauffeur, and technician. Weekends in Atlanta were hardly leisurely as she alternated between supporting her son and learning the skills necessary to keep him alive. Dressing, bathing, feeding, bowel, bladder and skin care, suctioning mucous, performing muscle toning exercises, transportation, maintenance, and troubleshooting of all the equipment, even human physiology, were all included in her training regimen.

Fortunately for Barbara, her son was a person of no ordinary intelligence. Once his initial despondency began to lift, Brian's natural curiosity took over. Defying the medical model of the passive, compliant patient, he asked endless questions about his condition. It was not enough to tell him what to do. He demanded to know why.

The busy staff, unaccustomed to this level of interest, assumed he was being uncooperative. On occasion, they would casually chat over or around him as though he were absent. Such disregard made Barbara bristle. "Don't treat him like he's ignorant," she admonished them.

She appreciated that Brian's desire to understand his injury was integral to his recovery. For him, the correlation was clear: The more he grew to accept his disability, the more he wanted to know about it. By the time he was discharged from Shepherd Spinal Center, Brian Baco had absorbed enough medical information to make him something of an authority on the subject of quadriplegia.

Brian's education and training included his new mode of transportation, a technological chariot known as the sip and puff wheelchair. By alternately sucking on (sipping) and blowing into (puffing) twin tubes positioned at his mouth, he could move right or left, backward or forward with surprisingly fine precision. His new wheelchair also came equipped with an apparatus that enabled him to shift positions. He was taught to periodically use his mouth to activate the electronic mechanism that tilted his seat and redistributed his weight to protect vulnerable pressure points.

The chair also became the object of a mini-drama during his recovery. His insurance company rejected the initial request for $10,000 to purchase the sip and puff wheelchair, having determined that it was unnecessary equipment. The company was prepared instead to pay only for a *manually* operated chair, which, of course, was useless to a person with paralyzed arms.

Equipped with this technology, Brian stood to retain a measure of personal freedom. Without it, he was doomed to even greater dependence and indignity. Shepherd's case management team, well versed in the ways of the insurance industry, refused to discharge Brian for an entire month until the insurance provider finally capitulated. A $10,000 wheelchair begins to look like a bargain compared with what was at the time $30,000 worth of rent at Shepherd.

Another important part of the rehabilitation process was to stabilize Brian's breathing. Many individuals with such catastrophic injuries are still receiving supplemental oxygen by mouth at the time of their admission to Shepherd. The staff must wean them of this dependence by addressing their fears about the reliability of respirators. As their confidence in the respirator grows, a patient's need for supplemental oxygen usually disappears.

Depending on the severity of the injury to the spine, patients may retain some control over the muscles in their neck. By exercise and practice, these muscles can often be utilized to promote accessory breathing that allows the patient to remain independent of the life support system for minutes at a time.

During Brian's stay at Shepherd, the staff experimented with what is called phrenic nerve pacing. The phrenic nerve regulates breathing by relaying signals from the brain to the muscles of the diaphragm. By stimulating this nerve with electric impulses, some patients can learn to breathe on their own for short periods. But neither of these treatment options proved successful with Brian.

Restoring Brian's speech was an additional priority. Audible sounds are a function of air being directed across the surface of the vocal cords. Deprived of air, the victim is incapable of speech. Respirator-dependent patients have a couple of options available for supplying oxygen to their lungs. Some prefer to wear an oxygen mask, which has obvious practical as well as aesthetic disadvantages. Others choose a tracheotomy by which a surgical procedure (tracheostomy) opens a hole in the throat at the trachea. The hole is fitted with a plastic rim. A plastic tube is then threaded through the center hole of the rim and brought to rest at the trachea as a means of delivering oxygen to the lungs.

Since the air flowing through the tracheotomy bypasses the vocal cords, patients on respirators speak only as they exhale. During conversation, conspicuous pauses in the middle of a sentence are not uncommon as the speaker must stop to allow the respirator to refill his or her lungs.

At first, the tracheostomy left Brian mute. Unable to speak or gesture with his hands, he resorted to silently mouthing words as his only means of communication. His daily regimen included training with a speech therapist to learn the mechanics of speaking with the assistance of his respirator. The trick, as he soon learned, was to synchronize exhaling air with enunciating words. Finally, on July 9, which also happened to be his sixteenth birthday, Brian uttered his first audible sounds.

But the greatest challenge of the rehabilitation process was mental. There could be no real physical recovery from such a severe injury. Brian's survival would largely depend on accepting the limitations of his impairment and reclaiming the will to live. Shepherd was sensitive to Brian's precarious emotional state and provided him with support groups, peer support furnished by other disabled people, and a weekly consultation with a social worker. Every effort was made to normalize his life as much as possible, from assigning a teacher to help him with his schoolwork, to offering him sex education to help him cope with his impaired condition.

But in the end, no one, no matter how conscientious and committed, could re-ignite his passion for life and restore his will to live. That he would have to discover for himself. And since pre-existing issues tend to get magnified in a person's disability, his strength of character was about to be tested as it never had before.

Chapter 11

In the Atlanta of the '60s and '70s, with its booming commerce and boundless vitality, building codes were generally oblivious to issues of accessibility. Neither architects nor contractors appreciated that steps, cramped bathrooms, and narrow thresholds were all impediments to wheelchair-bound citizens. In truth, the disabled were anonymous. Without a forum, they remained an invisible minority in those places where public policy was set. From that inhospitable setting Dave Webb emerged as a point man demanding fair and equal treatment for his disabled brothers and sisters.

Dave's neck was also broken in a diving accident at age fifteen, and he, too, was diagnosed a C-5 quadriplegic, though the injury to his spine never worsened. Yet what began as a senseless calamity for him transformed itself into the defining event of Dave's life. Surviving nearly forty years of quadriplegia until his death some years ago of cancer, he became Atlanta's most recognizable disabled citizen, as well as its most outspoken advocate for the rights of the disabled. His efforts eventually resulted in his appointment to committees that worked on revising building standards and raising awareness within the construction industry on issues of accessibility.

After Dave and his allies established a beachhead for their grievances, ramps began to appear at the entrances of buildings and curb cuts at street crossings. With every public meeting Dave attended, every task force on which he served, and every awards ceremony where he posed for pictures, acknowledgement of the plight of disabled citizens in Atlanta grew. Driving around town in a former bread truck that his father had specially customized for him, Dave became a hero to those who felt marginalized and a thorn in the side of those who opposed his efforts as costly and intrusive.

In the process of all this, Dave managed to craft a remarkably "normal" life for himself. He graduated from law school, practiced law within the banking industry, and even courted a woman who would later become his wife. He also served on a White House task force appointed by his personal acquaintance, President Jimmy Carter. The spinal injury endowed him with his life's work, precipitated his participation in the founding of the nationally recognized Shepherd Spinal Center, and gained him access to influential people. Recognized by the Jaycees as one of the ten outstanding young men in America, he transformed his broken neck into an asset for himself and other disabled people.

For almost four decades, Denny Webb watched and absorbed the lessons of his older brother's journey. He was astounded by the inner strength Dave displayed as well as the vibrant life he fashioned for himself. But Denny also came to appreciate the price it exacted in countless hardships and indignities. It was the side of disability the public did not see that transformed members of the Webb family, including Denny. Tasks as mundane as eating, going to the bathroom, and dressing were Dave's daily ordeal. Just getting out of bed each morning took ninety minutes.

Before public access became law, Denny witnessed many occasions when his brother's tenacity and ingenuity helped him enter a building that appeared inaccessible to the handicapped. If the front door was blocked by steps, Dave searched the perimeter of the building for a barrier-free kitchen or service entrance. Sometimes there was none. While attending law school in a building with no elevator, he recruited classmates to hoist him and his electric wheelchair, with a combined weight of 400 pounds, up a flight of stairs each day to attend classes.

But Denny also noted the physical toll the disability took on his brother. The constant pressure on Dave's buttocks wore hideous ulcers into his flesh and nearly to the bone. While incapable of feeling the pain from those sores, he suffered terribly from the infections they caused. The cancer that eventually claimed his life was believed to have begun with those wounds that would not heal.

Denny Webb, who like his brother was a prominent Atlanta attorney, first learned of Brian Baco while Dave was receiving treatment at Shepherd in 1986. One day, he stopped by to visit and was introduced to Barbara, who was visiting in Dave's room at the time. Denny accompanied her down the hall to meet Brian. After talking for a short time, Denny surmised that the boy possessed many of the qualities he found most admirable in his own brother.

But it was the contrast in the circumstances of their respective lives that struck him most deeply. Where Dave's condition was disturbing, Brian's was dismal. Where Dave could drive his own van, Brian was struggling simply to draw a breath. Denny appreciated that his brother had prevailed because of the strength of his character, the love and support of his family, access to adequate resources, and the fact that his injury did not deprive him of his personal freedom or self-determination. Remove any one of these factors from the equation, and the outcome might have been different.

Denny could see that Brian possessed the inner strength and support of his family to fashion a rewarding life for himself. But he realized that with the ascension of Brian's injury to the C-2 level, the prospects for a successful adjustment had grown dimmer. He recognized that even a boy as gifted as Brian would be hard pressed to cope with the lifetime of dependence, confinement, and deprivation stretching out before him.

"Life on a respirator," he admits, "is about as terrible as any I've ever seen."

As Barbara recounted the events that had brought them to that unenviable place, Denny began to construct some theories. The deterioration in Brian's condition so soon after the surgery on his neck raised suspicion in his legally trained mind. Was there a cause-and-effect relationship between the two?

The impairment was permanent. There was no restoring what

function Brian had lost. But if there was evidence of negligence by the surgeon or the hospital staff, then Denny believed that person or persons should be held accountable and the family compensated for their loss.

At the same time, Denny Webb is no ambulance chaser. Years of litigation have enabled him to build a successful law practice based on referrals. Ironically, his practice has thrived on defending clients, including physicians, against malpractice suits. Unlike some of his less established colleagues, he can afford to be selective about who he represents. For instance, he seldom represents plaintiffs in lawsuits, explaining, "A lawyer who does that kind of work ends up with many clients you don't like." He only crosses over to the plaintiff's side of the courtroom if he is either interested in the merits of the case or feels affinity for the people involved. In Brian's case, both criteria were met. He found their complaint compelling, and he liked the Bacos as people.

With Barbara's permission, Denny obtained a copy of Brian's medical records from Spartanburg General Hospital, and in early November 1986, while Brian was completing his rehabilitation at Shepherd, Denny contacted Dr. George Udvarhelji, a retired professor of neurosurgery at Johns Hopkins, and asked him to offer an opinion about possible negligence on the part of the attending physician.

Udvarhelji's examination of the medical records and subsequent consultation with Denny confirmed the attorney's suspicion. Although the surgeon's justification for the surgery was to stabilize the patient, there was nothing in either the doctor's or the nurses' progress notes to indicate instability prior to surgery. In fact, the notes suggested Brian's condition was stable by the time he was admitted to the hospital and remained so until the time of his operation. It was ten hours post-surgery that the first written documentation appears that his condition was deteriorating.

Udvarhelji believed that operating on a spine already severely traumatized was unnecessarily aggressive and put the patient at risk to suffer even further damage to the area. For years, he had taught his medical students to immobilize patients with spinal cord injuries in a brace, and postpone surgery for up to ten days to allow for a thorough evaluation. In his estimation, the surgeon, Dr. Calvert McCorkle, had indeed deviated from standard procedure.

Armed with the ammunition he needed, Denny proposed the Baco family file a lawsuit charging McCorkle with medical malpractice. He agreed to try the case on a contingency basis, meaning that he would only collect his third of the proposed million-dollar settlement if he won the case. If the case was lost, however, he would absorb the estimated $60,000 in expenses it would cost him to try it.

Denny contends that the material gain was not a priority to him in this case. Decades of living with his brother's quadriplegia had tweaked his sensibilities to human suffering. He understood that Brian, like Dave, "did not see what we see." Other attorneys may have accepted the Bacos' case, but none could match Denny's unique qualifications or perspective for trying it. The recollection of his own family's hardship ensured the Bacos impassioned representation in the courtroom.

The case also appealed to Denny's sense of fair play. He sincerely believed the surgeon's impatience had done grievous harm to Brian, and he was determined to extract some monetary award to compensate Brian and his family.

The contingency arrangement was the only way Barbara could afford to take the matter to court. The family's modest budget could not absorb tens of thousands of dollars in legal fees. Nor was legal action something Barbara had ever seriously considered as a solution to her family's woes.

Barbara admits she was suspicious at first of Denny's offer. She consulted with lawyers she knew in Spartanburg who warned that it would be difficult to successfully sue a doctor in South Carolina courts. Yet, ultimately, the offer of high-powered legal representation at no personal cost proved too tempting to decline.

Barbara, who harbored a grudge against McCorkle for his handling of the case, was eager to confront him in court. She had not forgotten his lack of availability or how he discharged Brian without so much as a single expression of sympathy for the unfortunate turn of events.

She also remembered that on the night her son was placed on life support, no one bothered to notify her of his deteriorating condition.

The lawsuit would offer her family a possible opportunity to avenge these perceived wrongs. And while there was no such thing as equitable compensation for all Brian had lost, the monetary award would at least underwrite some of the things insurance had denied them, such as remodeling the bathroom to make it accessible for his use. Upon further consideration, Barbara, with Herman's blessings, decided to accept Denny's invitation.

With Brian's rehabilitation nearing completion and the insurance carrier at last cooperating in procurement of the wheelchair, Barbara and Brian anticipated his discharge.

The five and a half months of weekend travel and living out of a suitcase had left Barbara weary. Even her old Celica finally broke down and died of fatigue, though friends in Spartanburg generously donated money to revive it. Their charitable gesture notwithstanding, the backbreaking schedule left her financial, emotional, and physical reserves depleted. So it was with great relief that she bid Atlanta farewell.

As for Brian, his emotional state began to brighten as the date of his discharge approached. After months of enduring institutional life, he longed to return to the familiar surroundings of his hometown.

Yet he could not fathom what awaited him. Sleepy Spartanburg had changed little during his absence. Brian, on the other hand, had undergone a radical transformation. He might just as well have been an immigrant arriving at some foreign port of entry, so different was his perspective from that of the able-bodied people who would gather to celebrate his return. In their understandable eagerness to flee Atlanta, neither mother nor son was prepared to see what would later become all too apparent: Shepherd Spinal Center had become more of a home than Spartanburg ever would be again.

Chapter 12

Four years from now I see myself either thanking someone for a job, or trying to continue my schooling . . . Thereafter, my path gets cloudy. I cannot foresee it, but marriage is a possibility. There are many possibilities, and trying to foresee them all would make winning the lottery child's play. I only plan to do the best I can, for I will always remember a young man, with his entire future ahead of him, losing that future, and gaining mine.

Brian Baco wrote these words for a high school English assignment. They seem to indicate that the rehabilitation at Shepherd had achieved its desired objective. The black cloud of despair that enveloped him since the night of the accident had apparently given way to a small but pure ray of hope. His renewed sense of optimism called him back to Spartanburg with the possibility of a future stirring once more in that fertile mind of his.

His hometown is a city with a population of about 45,000 located in the northwest corner of South Carolina at the foot of the Blue Ridge Mountains. Once a center of textile manufacturing, many of its mills have closed in recent decades due primarily to increases in cheaper imported goods and outsourcing of jobs. As a consequence, the community has had to rebuild its economic base through greater industrial diversification.

Textiles have been replaced by dozens of national and international companies that have located in the area, drawn there by the absence of labor unions, a good location along the busy I-85 corridor between Atlanta and Charlotte and a pro-business climate.

In many respects, Spartanburg is a quintessential southern town working to rouse itself from its segregated past. The city has had a black mayor and police chief in the last decade but still remains largely divided along racial lines. Low-income blacks are concentrated in the urban core, while whites are more likely to live in the more affluent suburbs.

Large, prominent Protestant churches still dominate Spartanburg's downtown skyline. It is inhabited by people with rock solid conservative values. That cultural climate makes it an ideal place to raise a family, but it can be a lonely one for individuals with unconventional ideas or lifestyles.

Brian's return to Spartanburg would reveal all that is best about small town life. His hometown paper, the Spartanburg Herald-Journal, published his story and his school picture on its front page, which galvanized the public's response. The Spartanburg community quickly mobilized itself and delivered a flurry of charitable gestures.

A local bar collected several thousand dollars from its patrons to defray expenses the family incurred during the stay at Shepherd. David Gillespie, a complete stranger to the family, spearheaded the drive to establish the "Brian Baco Relief Fund" that raised $13,000 toward the purchase of a van specially modified to provide for Brian's transportation needs. The local Ford dealership did their part, too, discounting the sticker price of the vehicle. Other area organizations, including Brian's high school, lined up to sponsor a series of charitable events. The Vocational Rehabilitation Center donated labor and materials to build a ramp at the house where Brian would live and widened the doorways to accommodate his wheelchair.

When Brian's entourage finally eased into the driveway at Runnymeade Drive in a borrowed van on Thanksgiving Day 1986, neighbors were on hand to assure him a warm reception. A welcoming banner and Thanksgiving dinner were waiting on them, as well as a nurse and the necessary equipment required for Brian's care.

With goodwill raining down on them and Brian more content than she had seen him at any time since the accident, Barbara permitted herself a momentary indulgence of cautious optimism—perhaps out of her son's bleak misfortune he might yet manage to scratch out a satisfactory life for himself.

But the reunion with the house at 103 Runnymeade Drive was no cause for celebration where she was concerned. The residence she had once shared with Herman and the boys represented the prison of an unhappy marriage that Barbara had worked so hard to escape. At the time of their separation, she first found temporary accommodations in a nearby apartment. Later, when the two-bedroom house on White Oak Street appeared on the local real estate market, she couldn't resist the idea of home ownership and secured a bank loan to buy it.

The little house in the working class neighborhood was everything Barbara asked of it—the monthly payments were within her budget, and her name appeared exclusively on the mortgage. Signing the purchase contract and assuming the loan signified an important departure from her previous financial dependence on Herman.

No one was more surprised by her giddy new independence than Barbara herself. She landed a good position as the office manager for a local business called Computer Tymes. The salary provided her a measure of financial security and helped cement her resolve to buy the home. Buffeted for many months by a divorcing parent's guilt and grief about leaving her children, she gradually began to regain her equilibrium. At just past forty years old, Barbara was busy rebuilding a new life for herself as a professional single woman.

That newfound autonomy collapsed, however, under the imposing weight of her son's accident. As a result of an owner buy-out as well as her preoccupation with Brian's care, Barbara eventually lost her job at Computer Tymes. She had to settle instead for a less lucrative position in the corporate accounting department of a nearby engineering firm. The modest hourly wage she earned did not pack the same purchasing punch of her previous salary, and belt-tightening measures became necessary. Her descent accelerated with the realization that the spacious house on Runnymeade Drive was more accommodating of Brian's special needs than her own home. The work to widen doorways inside the house guaranteed Brian access to four rooms as well as the backyard deck.

Only by a stroke of misfortune was the house still available to the family. Herman, who had been unable to sell it since leaving the town the year before, was stuck with the monthly mortgage. So, the subsequent decision to move Brian there required very little deliberation. Herman tacitly blessed the arrangement by continuing to pay the mortgage, while Barbara reluctantly rented out her own home on White Oak Street and moved in with her son.

Following many months of painful dislocation, Brian was bound for the only home he had ever known—a comfortable, ranch-style dwelling nestled in the quiet, middle-class subdivision of Camelot. Brian was pleased by the reunion with his old neighborhood. And the house's convenient location near his high school meant his classmates could drop by to see him after their classes.

Barbara, however, was left with conflicting emotions. The return to Runnymeade represented a major concession to all she had opposed in her former marriage. She found herself once again financially bound to Herman, living in his home, and dependent on his insurance to pay the bills for Brian's care. Only great love for her son made it possible for her to swallow such a bitter concession.

To prepare the house for Brian, a hospital bed replaced the living room furniture. The decision to locate him in the largest, most accessible space made sense from a practical perspective. But it also served as a metaphor. As the first thing you saw upon entering the house and the last thing you saw on your way out the door, the bed's prominence symbolized the degree to which Brian's disability would come to monopolize the family's life. From the day he returned to the house, every decision, no matter how trivial, would revolve around Brian. His needs were—and had to be—Barbara's first priority. It was a reshuffling of family priorities that even Brian would grow to resent.

The sheer weight of the responsibility Barbara assumed soon began to exact a price. For all the inconvenience of trips back and forth to

Shepherd, she had been able to leave Atlanta on Sunday night assured her son was in capable hands. However, the return to Spartanburg quickly eroded that sense of well-being. Any illusions she may have entertained about caring for a quadriplegic were quickly swept aside by the enormous impracticality of it.

"All of a sudden this is more real than before, because now you're totally responsible. . .[you] had to know everything you needed to know to keep him alive," she says of that adjustment period.

In the months following the accident, a recurring nightmare plagued Barbara. As Brian's lifeless body lays on a gurney in the waiting room at Shepherd, an attendant stands nearby holding her son's decapitated head in his hands.

"That belongs to Brian," says Barbara, reaching out to retrieve what remains of her son.

"I know," replies the attendant, pulling it just out of reach of her outstretched hands.

"Well, just what are you planning to do with it?" she asks, in an exasperated tone.

"We cut it off because it's the only part of him that still works."

The dream was a parable of her loss as well as his. Yet out of that loss, a daily routine gradually began to emerge. On weekdays, Barbara rose by 6:00 a.m. to prepare Brian for the first-shift nurse who arrived at 7:00. After returning home from work in the evening, there was dinner to prepare and chores to complete. The hour from 9:00 to 10:00 each evening was reserved for tending to his personal hygienic needs. Guests who were present in the home during that hour were expected to leave or to at least make themselves scarce. Mucous had to be suctioned from his throat and range-of-motion exercises were forced upon his withered limbs.

For Brian, quadriplegia complicated even bodily responses as basic as bowel and bladder activity. He was catherized, which meant each night the bag in which his urine collected had to be emptied and the catheter cleaned. Unable to expel his own excrement, Barbara donned latex gloves, digitally stimulating his unresponsive bowels and manually removing and disposing of his stools. The task was unpleasant for her and mortifying for him. And at a stage of life when adolescents are notoriously self-conscious about their bodies, Brian suffered the regular indignity of being diapered by his mother.

Lacking the funds to remodel the family bathroom to make it accessible to him, Brian's bath each night consisted of a rinse with soapy water and a sponge. The sponge bath was more than a matter of simple hygiene, since damp, dirty skin encourages the formation of bedsores. His clothing and linens also had to be closely monitored for moisture and frequently changed throughout the day.

The care of a patient this profoundly injured is daunting because the demands are so relentless. To let up for even a single day was to risk endangering Brian's health and safety. The job made Barbara indispensable, offering her no vacation or sick leave, and rarely a day off.

The Bacos' home life was further complicated by the ongoing need to generate income. Brian could not be left alone during the day while his mother worked, nor could he be left in the care of just anyone.

Adult day care was not an option because its personnel lacked the necessary training to properly care for him. The same was true for sitters. Only persons with specialized training possessed the particular skills needed to tend to such an acute injury.

At first, home health providers managed his case, with nurses rotating in and out of the house in eight-hour shifts. But after three months, insurance restrictions reduced the staffing to two shifts of nurses per day.

According to Barbara, the new living arrangement took some getting used to: "Between learning to deal with a stranger in my house . . . and taking care of Brian, I think my insanity began."

Chapter 13

Finding and keeping qualified help proved to be a perpetual headache. The nurses supplied by home health care staffing agencies at the time were only loosely regulated by the state of South Carolina. This opened the door to entrepreneurs who eyed home health care as a lucrative, untapped market to exploit. Some of the marginal operations were long on volume but short on quality control.

In the first few years of his disability, Brian's insurance policy stipulated caregivers had to be either licensed or registered nurses. But without any state regulation to ensure compliance, the requirement had no real teeth. Review of the personnel assigned to Brian's case paints a dismal picture of incompetence that Barbara indelicately describes as "some sorry-ass people."

Deborah Seay, who would become one of Brian's favorite nurses, had formerly worked as a technician in a hospital drawing blood. By the time she arrived in the Baco residence, insurance standards had been relaxed to the point that certified nursing assistants were permitted to work private duty. With only six weeks of formal training under her belt, Deborah was qualified, according to state and industry standards, for assignment to a respirator-dependent quadriplegic.

Given the poor professional standards, the Runnymeade Drive address resembled a revolving door of employment. Nurses came and, invariably, nurses went.

The stories that family and friends recount of the lack of

professionalism seem unconscionable. Some were dismissed for coming to work intoxicated, others for lying. One caregiver was fired for sleeping all day in an adjacent room, while another was dismissed because of a suspicion that she suffered from a mental illness.

An especially unpleasant episode involved $800 worth of items that mysteriously disappeared from the house. Barbara confronted the two nurses employed at the time, both of whom denied any knowledge of the missing items. When the police proposed that they submit to a polygraph test to clear themselves, both refused, and Barbara fired them.

Another nurse, for whom Barbara reserves special bitterness to this day, dropped Brian on the floor while moving him from his bed to his wheelchair. Others proved incapable of juggling the multitude of tasks the job demanded or were simply too indifferent to try. After Brian developed diabetes, samples of blood had to be drawn throughout the day to test his body's insulin level. Inexplicably, the nurse responsible for drawing the blood pricked the same swollen and inflamed fingers over and over again.

"How many fingers do you see?" asked Barbara, holding up both her hands.

"Ten," said the nurse.

"That means you have ten options for drawing his blood," she said. "I expect you to use all of them."

But perhaps the most grievous offense involved the condom catheter that was bound to Brian's penis with a Velcro strap. One morning, the nurse on duty secured the strap too tightly, turning it effectively into a tourniquet. The nurse then compounded her mistake by violating a cardinal sin of her discipline—failure to inspect her work. Deprived of its blood supply an entire day, layers of skin on his penis died and had to be surgically removed in yet another insult to his manhood.

Deborah Seay contends that most of the patients she served prior to Brian were near death either due to terminal illness or old age. Unconscious or otherwise too incapacitated to protect themselves, such individuals are easy prey for incompetent or unethical caregivers.

Brian, on the other hand, was fully conscious and demanded a level of attention to which many of these nursing assistants were unaccustomed. In his company, their liabilities were exposed for the safety risk they represented. If his respirator malfunctioned and the nurse on duty failed to respond promptly and decisively, he could easily die of suffocation. But perhaps even crueler than the physical danger was the fact that each of these incidents reinforced Brian's perception that the people who were his companions most of his waking hours really didn't give a damn about him.

In fairness, it should be said that the nurses were not without grievances of their own. They were no doubt put off by spells when Brian was uncooperative and temperamental. The need for privacy, so crucial to his well-being, posed a bind for them. The nurses were expected to tend to his care while at the same time honoring his demand to be left alone. Efforts to perform their duties were often greeted irritably as unwelcome interruptions of his solitude. Whenever the weather permitted, Brian preferred to be wheeled outside to a favorite spot in the backyard beneath a large oak tree. It was understood that the nurse was to remain inside and out of sight. A baby monitor was attached to his chair to listen for signs of distress.

Brian's initial reaction to the nursing staff had been hostile. He resented the invasion of privacy, a feeling matched for its intensity only by the loathing he saved for his own impotence. It was as much that sense of helplessness as their incompetence that made his caregivers convenient targets for his scorn. He was utterly dependent on them for even the simplest of tasks. For instance, if he wished to read, the nurse had to be nearby to turn the pages. When a bodily function needed tending or he was hungry, they became his hands and feet.

The circumstances that brought Brian and his caregivers together represented a perfect formula for misery for everyone. His daily companions were people he did not choose and would never have chosen under more ordinary circumstances. They were selected for him by availability rather than compatibility. Brian grew so contemptuous of a particular weekend nurse that Barbara was afraid to leave him alone with her.

Indignant about a work ethic she regarded as sloppy and unprofessional, Barbara adopted a confrontational approach with the staff. Some quit under the strain of her scrutiny, while others were fired. "It was always starting all over again," she says.

She was also dismayed to discover that the reinforcements were usually unprepared for caring for a patient with Brian's special disabilities. The staffing agencies generally failed to deliver on their guarantees to provide qualified personnel. A warm body was about all she could count on. Consequently, introducing Brian's regimen of care to new nurses invariably got deferred to Barbara, a woman already shouldering an exceptional burden of cares.

The level of general incompetence she witnessed made Barbara shudder. Each morning during the week, she left home quite literally placing her son's fragile life in the hands of a person, very often a stranger, whose trustworthiness was suspect. She recalls occasions where she had no choice but to hurriedly explain Brian's care to a new nurse before rushing off to work. If an emergency arose for which the nurse was unprepared or inattentive to, he could be dead before Barbara reached home.

Yet Barbara remained resolute about the expectations for her son's care. She watched for nurses who were competent, reliable, and, most of all, compassionate human beings. She could teach the requisite skills if she could find a person with the potential to be an appropriate companion. That person had to possess the inner strength to tolerate Brian's dark spells, a person with enough perspective and self-confidence to realize his fluctuating moods reflected the impossibility of his circumstances more than a personal slight. Surely, she reasoned, what she asked was no more than any conscientious parent would expect for her child.

Chapter 14

Eventually, Barbara's persistence paid off in the person of Ruby Craig, whose arrival in the Baco household signaled a positive shift in their fortunes. Ruby is a pleasant, unpretentious woman with a large and generous presence. She laughs easily and often, especially at her own shortcomings, oozes common sense, and is nonchalant about the steady parade of visitors in and out the door.

One room of her small home is a studio where portraits of her offspring (nine children and more than twenty grandchildren) are displayed. It is difficult to distinguish where her role as a mother ends and her responsibilities as a grandmother begin. She seems to regard every generation of her family with the same kind, matriarchal eye.

Ruby began years ago as a nursing assistant, sometimes called a sitter or aid. But hungry for greater responsibility and earning power, she returned to the local technical college and earned a degree as a licensed practical nurse. After completing her education, she initially contracted with staffing agencies where the opportunities to work were plentiful. She later abandoned that work in favor of employment at nursing homes. It was through her experience with these agencies that she first acquired a preference for private duty nursing, where the extended length of care offered her an opportunity to build close relationships of a kind that were unlikely to develop as a floor nurse.

The coffee table of her living room holds a photo album of

patients she has served on private duty. Showing me the photos, she beams with the same pride and affection as she does when speaking of her own kin, clear evidence of a woman with a boundless capacity to care for and form attachments to people. Ruby is intriguing in her defiance of a discipline that calls for maintaining a degree of professional detachment. She lives, instead, in a world where the boundaries between supposed personal and professional standards get blurred. She does not so much pull a shift as she adopts a patient and his family into her sphere.

One portion of her photo album is devoted to memorabilia she collected while caring for Brian Baco. From the day she first appeared at the front door on Runnymeade Drive, her work ethic and attitude would distinguish her from so many who had come before her. Ruby's gift for relationship building provided a refreshing change for a family accustomed to far less. The positive impact she had on a beleaguered Barbara was both immediate and profound. Here, at last, was someone who regarded her son as more than a paycheck. Instead, Ruby approached this case as her personal mission. Armed with wit and down-home charm, she infiltrated and ultimately wore down the resistance of a mother and son resigned to disappointment.

For Brian, Ruby's arrival was startling as well. She was the first nurse who showed genuine interest in him as a person. Not only did she carry out her duties competently, she was sensitive to his feelings. Everything about her suggested that she actually liked him. For the first time since the accident, his days were more than stupefying and dreary. As daily companions, they played, teased, and, best of all, laughed with one another. Like any family, they had their spats. And like any family, they made up. She cooked for him and corrected him when he was surly. She studied his moods and learned when to push him as well as when to leave him alone. Her vast experience as the mother and grandmother of teens, along with her innate people skills, informed the relationship she shared with her young patient. Rather than relating to him as a fragile invalid, Ruby treated Brian as she would any of her "young 'uns." And he, in turn, responded to her positively.

"She made him laugh and laugh," says Barbara. "And he loved her."

During their four years together, he grew to appreciate her as both a parental figure and a friend. In time, their relationship evolved to such a high level of comfortable familiarity that he preferred Ruby, rather than his mother, tend to his most intimate needs.

When Herman invited Brian to visit in Pensacola, Brian only consented to make the trip after Ruby agreed to accompany him. She set aside her personal life for an entire month so as not to disappoint him. The fact she agreed to go to Florida was no more impressive than the fact he would ask. Apart from Barbara, no other person would figure so prominently or come to mean so much to Brian's survival as Ruby Craig.

For a weary and wary Barbara, Ruby's arrival provided the support for which she was so desperate. At last she had found an ally she could trust implicitly, someone whose very presence helped dispel the fear that had preoccupied her. With Ruby on the job, Barbara could leave the house confident her son would be properly cared for.

Furthermore, she was buoyed by the knowledge that Brian finally had a true companion to make his impossible existence more bearable. Over the course of her association with the Bacos, Ruby did not so much work for the family as she lived with them. Volunteering for assignments that far exceeded her duties and ones others would regard as demeaning, she cooked, cleaned, ran errands, and served as social director. In essence, she became the matron of the Baco home. And each day, in a multitude of ways great and small, tangible and intangible, she endeared herself to the Baco family.

Ruby was also instrumental in Brian's decision to venture out from his home for the first time as a quadriplegic. She proposed that they christen the new Ford van specially equipped for him by taking it to a local steakhouse for dinner. But Brian, who had lived safely ensconced in the cocoon of his Runnymeade home, balked at the idea. Still painfully self-conscious about his disability, he was intimidated by the thought of people staring at him. But Ruby refused to back down. Convinced that Brian must address this fear quickly if he was to stand a chance at a decent life, she gently yet methodically wore down his resistance.

"Don't you want to get you one of those big ole' T-bones and a baked potato?" she asked.

He looked away, trying to ignore her.

"Come on now, Brian," she coaxed. "I know good and well you'd love to have a steak."

He continued to look away.

"Brian?" she said again more emphatically while stretching her head out to re-enter his field of vision.

Slowly, a faint smile creased his lips, and she smiled back, knowing she had him.

After they returned home from the restaurant, Ruby playfully teased Brian.

"So Brian, exactly how many people did you see staring at you?" she asked.

"None," he said as a big, sheepish grin spread across his face.

That evening was to represent an epiphany. To be sure, there would be instances of insensitivity and even occasional blatant cruelty that most disabled people have suffered, but gradually, under Ruby's tutelage, Brian was learning to believe in himself again.

With Ruby at the wheel and Brian in the back, his chair anchored to the floor by chains, the van shuttled the two of them to malls, movies, restaurants, and ballgames. That is not to suggest these excursions with him were ever easy. To transport a quadriplegic from one place to another, especially one who would eventually weigh more than two hundred pounds, required an unusual amount of advance preparation and care. Just loading Brian in the van was an adventure. Without the use of arms or legs to protect him from falls, he lived in fear his wheelchair would overturn while he was being raised and lowered on the van's hydraulic lift.

There was also the challenge of making his way around an able-bodied world indifferent to him. I once accompanied Brian and Barbara for an appointment at his doctor's office where his wheelchair dominated the floor space, transforming an ordinarily spacious waiting room into a congested obstacle course. But Brian, with the skill of a truck driver backing his rig into a loading dock, used alternating sips and puffs to expertly navigate his wheelchair through the maze.

On their trip to Pensacola, Brian asked Ruby if they could spend a day at the beach. The outing was not practical since Pensacola's beaches were not handicapped accessible at the time, but Ruby, who insisted Brian's life be as normal as possible, could not bring herself to refuse him. Making their way down to the beach, they struck an image that was as preposterous as it was sad—of a large, black woman laboring in the hot Florida sun, determined beyond reason to move a white kid in a wheelchair across an impossibly uncooperative stretch of soft sand. Ruby alternately pushed and dragged Brian a short distance before the wheels would become buried in the sand. By exerting her weight, as well as her will, against the chair, she managed to free the wheels just enough to move him forward short distance before they became buried all over again. After many rounds of struggle, she succeeded, at last, in perching Brian's chair on the crest of a dune. From that vantage point, he was able to survey the surf even if he would never again know the sensation of the waves breaking against his body.

Ruby also came to be appreciated by Brian's friends. While she bantered easily with the kids, it was her cooking—a cultural marriage of Southern and soul food—that his friends, especially the boys, came to admire the most. Tempted by a cuisine that featured fried meats, gravy, and biscuits, Brian's buddies tried to time their visits to coincide with mealtime. Ruby seldom disappointed and could be counted on to set an extra place at the dinner table. In time, though, they came to take advantage of her hospitality, placing orders as though she was a short order cook. But Ruby Craig is no one's doormat.

One day when Bill Geen was visiting Brian, he made the mistake of pushing her too far.

"Say Ruby, how about some fried chicken and macaroni and cheese?" Bill asked. "Hey, you don't cook that stuff everyday!" she said, admonishing him.

Brian was fond of her talents in the kitchen, too. Like most males his age, he possessed a voracious appetite. For a period following the accident, it was suppressed by depression. But once he decided to live, he began to eat with a passion that never seemed satisfied. Food, everything from confections to casseroles, was a gift guests could bring on their visits to the Bacos' home that was sure to meet with Brian's approval. And as one of the few physical pleasures remaining to him, Barbara was reluctant to deny him.

But his appetite would ultimately prove to be a liability. Paralysis did not stunt his growth, so that by his late teens he had grown to over six feet tall and weighed well in excess of two hundred pounds. His growing girth made him more difficult to manage and promoted the development of bedsores. The excess weight also may have contributed to the onset of adult diabetes, a disease to which his family was already genetically predisposed.

Ruby shared Brian's passion for food, and together they elevated dining out to a sacrament. One of their favorite establishments was an anachronistic Spartanburg landmark called The Beacon, where authentic curb service has not managed to be replaced by a drive thru window. Its menu consists of traditional American fast food fare: burgers, fries, onion rings, and shakes. The fat content of Beacon food is of such legendary proportions that residents sometimes affectionately refer to it as "Gall Bladder City," and the clean up crew is known to spread sawdust on the floor to soak up the excess grease. Brian and Ruby, happily oblivious to counting fat grams, appreciated that virtually everything on the Beacon menu is served "a' plenty."

Their dining choices were often influenced as much by the quantity of the servings as by their quality. One evening, accompanied by Bill Geen, they commandeered a table at Shoney's, taking quite literally the promotion of "all-you-can-eat" shrimp. When the three hungry diners showed no sign of letting up, the waitress adopted a strategy to slow them down. She returned to their table each round with smaller and smaller portions. Finally, Ruby called her over to the table and proposed a truce:

"Here's the thing," she said, adopting her most diplomatic tone. "Doesn't that sign out there say 'all you can eat?'"

"Yeah," the waitress replied.

"Look, we don't want to mess with you. Just bring the shrimp, and we'll get out of here."

The plain talk worked. The waitress cooperated, and the three of them left the restaurant that night satisfied. But Ruby chuckles now recalling her boldness as well as amazement the restaurant's manager didn't give them the boot out the door.

Chapter 15

Ruby Craig eased the burden of providing for Brian's daily care. But Barbara's struggles with the temperamental technology keeping her son alive were just beginning.

Purchasing the equipment was an expensive proposition, but that was only the half of it. For all of its remarkable ingenuity, without routine maintenance and timely repairs, the technology was useless. A computer integrated into the wheelchair translated the sips and puffs of Brian's breath into electrical impulses that were transmitted as command signals to the moving parts of the chair. These commands enabled him to move forward and backward, to turn left and right and steer. But the technology was subject to limitations. The intricacies of its design made it susceptible to mechanical failure and more complicated and expensive to repair. The Bacos had to learn to live with these breakdowns that were frequent and expensive.

Although insurance technically covered the expense of servicing the equipment, Herman's policy was limited to $1 million on each of his dependents. Once that cumulative cap was reached, Brian's coverage would expire. While a million-dollar insurance policy is a comfortable safety net to most people, for a person with a disability as severe as Brian's, it felt less secure. Budgeting finite resources required some guesswork, as it was impossible to anticipate what his expenses would be or how long they would be needed. Would Brian survive for two years or for twenty? No one could say with certainty. So Barbara kept a running tab in her head, knowing that every single insurance claim she filed represented another drink from a trough that could not be replenished.

Servicing the wheelchair was further complicated because the only shop in the area qualified to work on it was thirty miles away. That meant Barbara had to leave work without pay for the sixty mile round trip to deliver the chair to the service center and then a second time to pick it up.

The demands of time and money would come to monopolize the family's decisions, forcing Barbara to make consistently difficult choices about how to appropriate scarce resources. During different periods of his disability, Brian was without the use of his van, wheelchair, or computer. The absence of any one of these heaped even more loss on a life that was already long on deprivation. When the wheelchair was out of commission, Brian remained in bed. When the van was in the shop, he stayed home. And when the computer needed repair, he simply did without.

The one indispensable piece of equipment, of course, was the respirator. Its uninterrupted operation preoccupied the waking thoughts of both mother and son. Brian's complete dependence on it could be compromised by either of two threats—a mechanical failure or a power outage. Power for his respirator was actually generated by two separate systems: an electrically powered unit by his bed and a battery powered unit attached to the wheelchair.

Both were designed to take ordinary room air, filter out the impurities and by means of a compression pump force that air through the plastic tubing attached to the trachea down into his lungs. For all its technological sophistication, artificial respiration cannot entirely compensate for the inability to breathe on one's own. The volume of air delivered by the pump was never sufficient to force full expansion of Brian's lungs. Consequently, the muscles of the diaphragm lost their tone and turned fibrous. The fibrosis gave Brian the distinctive barrel-chested appearance associated with those who suffer from asthma and other chronic breathing problems.

Since Brian could only speak while expelling air, his speech was synchronized with the operation of his respirator. A conversation with him resembled speaking with someone out of breath, the words coming out in staccato bursts that were regularly interrupted by pauses as he waited for the pump to deliver the next round of air to his lungs.

With its idiosyncratic lurches and pauses, a respirator can arouse anxiety in the uninitiated. Richard Mouzon, a rehabilitative psychologist who interviewed Brian, admitted that he feared the respirator might quit at any moment. Brian's attorney Denny Webb described the apparatus as unnerving. Denny's image of Brian as a person has faded with time, but the memory of the respirator, or that "awful thing," as he called it, remains vivid. A videotape of the wedding of a Baco family friend, with the distinct wheezing of the respirator in the background, retains to this day audio evidence of Brian's attendance.

But even for one as familiar with its operation as Barbara, the machine's temperament was a persistent source of worry. She feared she might sleep through its alarm if it went off in the middle of the night. To reassure herself, she practiced a nightly ritual of testing the alarm before heading off to bed.

After crawling into bed, she would lie awake late into the night, listening carefully for the incessant beeping of the machine that reassured her it was still working. Over time, she became so intimately acquainted with its operation that she was able to detect even the slightest variation in its rhythm.

At Shepherd, Brian had been taught to make a clicking sound with his tongue in the event his respirator failed. Used by dog owners to call their pets, this is one of the few audible sounds that a person can make without the help of the vocal chords. So conditioned was Barbara to listening for that particular cue, she went into a panic one day when a friend clicked her tongue to call for her dog. She became physically ill, abruptly excused herself, and refused to return to that person's house.

Actor Christopher Reeve has helped to popularize glossopharyngeal breathing, more commonly known as "frog breathing." Some high-level quadriplegics can compensate for the inactivity of their diaphragms by using the tongue like a piston to literally push air down the throat and into the lungs. The technique is non-instinctual, requiring practice and concentration to do effectively. But for those who manage to master it as Reeve has, frog breathing offers an added measure of independence as well as a reliable backup plan for mechanical failures.

Brian experimented with frog breathing, remaining off his respirator for as much as four minutes at a time. But the separation from life support provoked such intense feelings of anxiety in him that he eventually abandoned the practice.

Brian was even more apprehensive than his mother about the respirator's operation. Twice daily during the separation from his life support system, he relived the trauma of that night in the hospital when he was unable to breathe. The lingering memory of that night, combined with the helplessness of his predicament, compounded the dread he felt about death by asphyxiation.

Out of all those thousands of transfers, there was one occasion when his fear was realized. In anticipation of a trip to North Carolina to participate in Mike's wedding, Barbara made reservations with a Hampton Inn that advertised itself as handicapped accessible. But upon arriving at the motel and settling into their room, they discovered the bed's frame rested flush against the floor. The meaningless detail that would escape the attention of able-bodied people posed a major barrier to a person in Brian's condition. The mechanical lift that moved him from his chair into bed was equipped with wheels. The base of the lift was stabilized by wheeling it beneath the bed. Without adequate clearance, the equipment was useless.

Faced with the prospect her son would have to remain in his wheelchair the entire night, Barbara complained to the motel manager. He responded by providing a portable cot with the necessary clearance for the lift. But the cot created another hazard, introducing more clutter to a room that was already short on open floor space. Any object in the path of the lift presented an instant obstacle, slowing its progress and prolonging the time Brian would be disconnected from his respirator.

Gary Hyndman

With the help of David, who had accompanied the Bacos on the trip, Brian was settled safely into bed that night. However, the next morning during the transfer to his chair the plastic tubing became disconnected from the respirator. At first, Barbara had trouble locating the source of the failure. David recalls that his "blood turned cold" at the sight of his friend suddenly gasping for air. It was a terrifying moment, and one for which he was caught completely unprepared.

Seconds became critical. In a scene she had visualized many times in her head, Barbara thrust a strange instrument into David's hands and shouted instructions on how to operate the ambu bag. Meanwhile, Barbara scrambled around on the floor, finally managing to pinpoint and correct the source of the problem.

For David, the image of his friend's panicstricken face remains fixed in his memory. For Brian, the incident further reinforced his fear of suffocation. But it was also a chilling reminder of his utter dependence on a machine that gave him life but could just as easily take it away.

Limited resources further compounded the family's woes. Barbara recalls an episode during a blackout caused by an electrical storm when Brian had to be transported to the hospital to access a life support system. En route, she used the ambu bag to manually pump oxygen into the lungs of her frightened son. The insurance company had previously denied her request for a backup generator to use in emergencies, citing it as another unnecessary expenditure. When it came to insurance, Barbara found herself standing in the shadow of a monolith she could not address, much less combat. Insurance practices were set in some distant corporate headquarters far removed from her son's intimate struggle for survival. The low-level personnel who responded to her appeals for help were as disposable and irrelevant as she felt. She ultimately resigned herself to the fact that the insurance provider was no ally.

Chapter 16

At first, Herman showed an interest in being supportive of his son. He maintained contact with Brian, though those contacts were often erratic. He phoned periodically, visited Spartanburg occasionally on weekends, and entertained Brian at his home in Florida for portions of the first two summers. But the Florida visits would not be sustained because Herman's apartment was not equipped to house a severely disabled person, and perhaps even more to the point, father and son were not close. The physical miles were less of a barrier than the emotional gulf separating them. In time, it felt less awkward being apart than it did coming together.

Dean lived with his mother and brother in Spartanburg for the first year of Brian's disability, but his supervision eventually proved too much for Barbara to handle.

"He was determined not to do what was expected of him," she says.

Dean's uncooperative nature incurred her wrath, and she lashed out angrily at him. He responded with even more belligerence and defiance. He taunted and tormented Brian, triggering conflict that often made it impossible for them to occupy the same room.

One day, for example, Dean switched off the television while Brian was watching it, a gesture coldly calculated to incite his older brother.

"Turn the damn television back on!" Brian shouted.

"Turn it back on yourself," said Dean, taunting his brother's disability.

Lacking both the patience and stamina to deal with her troubled child, Barbara eventually shipped Dean back to Herman in Florida. But the change of locale made little difference as Dean continued to spin out of control, lost in a spiral of drug abuse and truancy.

On Brian's return to Spartanburg, the local media gushed about his heroic effort to survive. During his first days at Shepherd Spinal Center, a story appeared on the front page of the daily newspaper quoting Barbara as saying: "That's what they teach them here; that they are still the same persons, that they can accomplish most any dreams they want to accomplish. They teach them to live to their limits."

That hopeful message, for which everyone had waited, seemed to galvanize the community into action. A parade of friends and even strangers streamed to the house on Runnymeade to offer their encouragement accompanied by their extravagant promises to stay in touch. The jersey Brian wore as a member of the high school soccer team was officially retired during a ceremony before a game. By their verbal and material support, the citizens of Spartanburg expressed their collective desire for Brian to live among them, and, at least in the early stages, made good on their pledge to help the family adjust.

Inspired by the community's blessings, Brian responded with a commitment of his own. Despite the obvious limitations of his condition, he set out with firm resolve to rebuild his life. Barbara believes she and Brian were able to establish a tolerable routine because of her son's determination to make the situation work. His complaints, relative to the magnitude of the hardship he was asked to endure, were few. Mostly agreeable and polite, Brian came to appreciate that his personal misfortune did not justify inconveniencing others or making them unnecessarily uncomfortable.

In the four years Ruby was with him, Brian occasionally confided that his life was tiresome, but she says she seldom saw him "blue." His many admirers around town were unsparing in their praise for his spunk and grace. David marvels even now at how his friend was able to remain "so damn cheerful." His losses were great, yet Brian seemed determined that no one in his hometown would ever see him groveling in self-pity or bitterness.

Even though he was pronounced fit to return to school after his discharge from Shepherd in November, the lift on the school district's handicapped bus would not accommodate Brian's wheelchair, and the family van had not yet been purchased. An alternate plan was implemented by which Brian was taught at home by tutors.

Sean Cullen, David's father, was one of those who volunteered for the assignment. A native of Ireland, Sean is a scientist who prides himself on his fair and objective view of the world. But those qualities were to be challenged by what he witnessed at Shepherd Spinal Center. Until the day he accompanied his son to Shepherd Spinal Center to visit Brian, he had never laid eyes on him. Hearing David speak of Brian's condition was one thing; to witness his struggle to survive in person was something entirely different. The sight stirred a responsive emotional chord in Sean, and he vowed to do whatever he could to help.

Sean agreed to serve as Brian's physics tutor, a position for which his Ph.D. and years of professional experience in the field of applied mathematics easily qualified him. But from the outset, the pairing of these two individuals had to be based on something other than a natural affinity. The disparity in their ages was magnified by the obvious differences in their temperament. Brian's outgoing personality stood in contrast to Sean's reserve. Where Brian was playful, Sean is earnest. Where Brian was optimistic, Sean appears pensive. The two of them were not destined to recreate the kind of warm, filial bond Brian shared with Ruby. Instead, their relationship was to be defined by a mutual affection for and fascination with science.

Sean conscientiously appeared at the Bacos' residence once or twice a week for the next two years to provide instruction. A dry erase board was hung on the living room wall, and on it, Sean and Brian calculated solutions to equations that would make the average human brain ache.

Sean's challenge was to teach his student without the benefit of a laboratory where experiments could be conducted to demonstrate the abstractions of physics. But Brian soaked up the knowledge as he always had, leaving Sean so impressed by the young man's supple intellect and unusual aptitude for grasping complex concepts that he once pronounced him a "natural physicist."

Long after their physics lessons had ended, Sean received an unexpected phone call one evening from Barbara.

"Brian has been watching some show about Einstein's theory of relativity," she said.

"Oh, has he now?" replied Sean in his Irish brogue.

"I don't want to put you out, Sean. But he wanted me to ask if you would mind coming over and talking with him about Einstein's work."

As a scientist who has devoted his life to such inquiries, Sean was delighted to oblige. This curiosity was not uncommon in Brian, who seemed to thrive on contemplating life's weightier matters. Deprived of his physical freedom, what richness remained of Brian's life had to be mined from a vigorous commitment to his intellect. The quest for knowledge was one frontier his disability could not impede. He set out on this intellectual adventure with the same focus that once characterized his performance on the soccer field, eagerly digesting information and formulating opinions. Whether the subject was science or theology, politics or literature, evolution or economics, his musings about the world reflected a general suspicion of popular opinion and an uncompromising devotion to reason. The skepticism he expressed about such sacred American icons as capitalism and Christianity was unconventional, if not downright heretical. He was just as Sean had characterized him, a scientist at heart.

One summer afternoon Brian and I spent an hour talking about a wide array of topics. We spoke of the possibility of life on other planets, an idea that seemed plausible to him, before turning our attention to religion, a subject to which I have devoted the better part of my professional life.

"What do you think about the existence of God?" he asked.

"I'm not sure," I said. "People tend to think they know a lot more about God than we can actually know. The idea of God is too big for the human mind to comprehend."

"Yeah, that's what bothers me," he replied, warming up to the subject. "People just automatically say they believe in God because their family and everyone around them does. They don't think about what that means."

By the time we were done, I appreciated what Mike Burnette meant when he said he always looked forward to his visits with Brian because he was guaranteed a "great conversation." Our lively and evocative discourse that day didn't change the circumstances of Brian's life at all, but it did give me a glimpse inside that wonderful head of his. The irony was that by virtue of his irrepressible curiosity and willingness to challenge convention, Brian seemed more vitally alive than some of the people in the community determined to pity him.

Hoping to capitalize upon his student's strengths and reinforce his commitment to live, Sean Cullen and others obtained a personal computer for his home use. A local computer storeowner, Bill Tysinger, quietly donated the equipment and for years thereafter supplied the Bacos with free upgrades. Others in the community chipped in with hardware and software as well.

Proceeds from a fund-raising drive were applied toward the purchase of a stunning piece of engineering designed especially for those who have lost the use of their hands. This apparatus, that pre-dated voice activation technology, was called a keyboard emulator. It was optically activated by a penlight attached to a band fitted around Brian's head. The emulator board consisted of a series of slots, each corresponding to a key on a computer keyboard. A light activated sensor was located behind each slot. By maneuvering his head so that the beam of light fell upon the appropriate slot, Brian could activate the desired command on the keyboard.

The emulator board permitted him to compose letters, prepare homework assignments, compile a database, file information, access the Internet, and play computer games.

It was a case of love at first sight. Brian's raw analytical gifts corresponded perfectly to the computer's logic. Where most novices are intimidated by a computer's many functions, Brian took them on as a challenge. He immersed himself in its operations and succeeded in teaching himself sophisticated applications. In the language of *Zen*, he and the computer became one. Brian and Mike even learned to design their own computer programs.

Those closest to him were extremely grateful. The technology fulfilled at least two important purposes in Brian's life: First, it provided him a worthy outlet for exercising his active mind. A neighbor designed and constructed a desk that allowed him to maneuver his wheelchair directly in front of the monitor. Once the headband was fitted in place, Brian was free to disappear into the nether of cyberspace. Surfing bulletin boards and the Internet, this kid who was bound to a wheelchair was able to explore an expansive world of information and ideas. Whether communicating with other hackers around the country or downloading software, he would sit for hours transfixed before the monitor's glow. One evening, Barbara discovered him at the computer at midnight absorbed in a chess match with an opponent from New York.

Brian also developed a special fondness for virtual reality games that appealed to his active imagination and afforded him the vicarious sensation of movement. In addition, these games stoked the embers of what had once been a roaring competitive fire. He practiced relentlessly, mastering the necessary skills, until, as one friend remembers, "He could beat the socks off everyone who came in the house."

A particular favorite of Brian and his buddies was the bawdy "Larry the Lounge Lizard." The game's objective was to guide Larry, the slimy protagonist, in his conquests of a series of buxom blondes— a mission that earned high marks from a gang of perpetually horny adolescents. But it also appealed to the adults in Brian's life, who might have otherwise dismissed the game as either silly or offensive. They joined in the good-natured fun it aroused, grateful for anything that gave Brian even momentary enjoyment.

Secondly, the computer injected a healthy transfusion of self-confidence that the injury and nearly complete dependence on others had effectively eroded. Its mastery restored a semblance of Brian's former image of himself as a capable person.

The skills he developed manipulating the keyboard helped to realign a playing field that his disability had badly skewed. And in the process, he discovered a personal asset exceptionally prized by a culture just awakening to the potential of computer technology and growing increasingly more dependent on it. According to David, Brian embraced a basic maxim of the technology that escapes many users: "Computers, unlike people, always do as they are told."

Brian came to appreciate that most of the complaints about these machines are due to operator impatience and error, and that the secret to computer literacy involved making the initial investment in understanding how they work. As his skills developed, family and friends turned to him for help with computer problems that confounded them. And Brian was happy to oblige.

Yet his value as a computer consultant transcended sheer knowledge of their operation. It had as much to do with the patience and kindness he exhibited in working with individuals who sought his help. No matter how anxious or agitated they became, no matter how seemingly impossible the snarl, he refused to get rattled. Others sensed his confidence and under his calm, steady tutelage usually responded with increased competence at the keyboard. He managed to teach some of his nurses, many of whom had no previous exposure to computers, to navigate their way around a DOS filing system.

"He took me places on the computer I had never dreamed of," one friend recalls admiringly.

Chapter 17

Though not a religious person in the conventional sense, Brian had his own set of icons that he revered. One of these was a longstanding devotion to *Star Trek*. The first time we met, I quickly learned to tread lightly when it came to this subject.

"So, I understand you're a Trekkie," I said, launching into what I assumed was a safe conversation starter.

"I'm a Trekker," he snapped.

The intensity of his reaction caught me unprepared. As I was to later learn, the distinction is crucial. Costume-wearing, autograph-seeking, celebrity-ogling Trekkies are considered the lightweights of the Star Trek phenomenon. Trekkers, on the other hand, are its intelligentsia. The television program and its feature-length films represent the organizing principles of their lives. Some years ago, Barbara Adams achieved instant notoriety when she was seated as an alternate juror in the infamous Arkansas Whitewater Trial while wearing a Star Trek uniform in the courtroom. Asked by reporters about her unusual attire, she announced with the fervor of a born-again believer that it was to make manifest the show's wholesome values.

Barbara, David, and others watched Star Trek with Brian, but no one approached his passion for the program. The Baco household observed silence each evening between 10 and 11 when the local cable station broadcast syndicated reruns of the old series. Brian collected videotapes of favorite episodes, each of which he had seen countless times, and spoke fluently about their plots and themes. Brian, the Trekker, understood Star Trek's mission "to boldly go where no man has gone before" and took it as his own personal quest. Its portrayal of intergalactic space travel, technological advancement, and international cooperation all captivated his imagination.

An avid reader, Brian's taste in books paralleled his fascination with Star Trek. He enjoyed the writings of scientists such as Carl Sagan and Stephen Hawking, as well the science fiction of Isaac Asimov. He also adored fantasy novels, such as *The Illearth War Series* by Stephen R. Donaldson. The recurrent theme of this literary genre depicts the struggle between the human spirit and those forces that seek to subdue it—the inference to his personal experience being easily transparent.

But for all the years of his confinement, there was one type of book he could never abide. Occasionally, well-meaning individuals presented him with biographies of individuals who have "overcome" serious handicaps to lead happy, fulfilling lives. They were always politely received before later being shelved on a bookcase never to be opened. The motivation for presenting these books as gifts was born of the same miscalculation that repeated itself often in Brian's encounters with people who did not understand his condition. The clumsy attempts to make him feel better through motivational media and pep talks invariably backfired, leaving him to feel even greater inadequacy over an impairment against which he could not prevail. Implicit in that collection of books gathering dust on his bookcase was an essential life lesson: no human being possesses the power to dictate how another feels.

Of all Brian's interests, none was more ordinary than his love of competitive sports. Still an athlete in his head, he described for Barbara a series of recurring dreams in which he envisioned himself playing soccer while carrying his respirator in his hands. Weekends around the Baco household included a steady diet of televised games of football, baseball, and basketball, as well as boxing matches. These were accompanied by spirited debate about pivotal plays and key players. The University of South Carolina and the Oakland Raiders were two of his favorite teams.

Barbara did her best to encourage her son's interests. But the extraordinary circumstances that dominated Brian's life as a quadriplegic complicated their relationship immeasurably. Where once they had enjoyed the normal bond of a parent and child, the accident bound them together physically and emotionally in ways that would either transform their relationship or cause it to implode.

Friends who observed the two of them together falter now when attempting to put into words the exact nature of their bond. Some have called them best friends, while others compare them instead to a husband and wife. More than roommates, contextually different than spouses, they were a mother and child living under the same roof minus the normal hierarchical trappings of a family.

The image that lingers is of Brian in his hospital bed with Barbara perched at his side watching a boxing match together—a sport he adored and one she deplored. For her willingness to step outside the traditional maternal role and accept Brian on equal terms as an adult, she was rewarded with the pleasure of coming to know her son in a way many parents never experience their children. She proudly recalls occasions when he took her into his confidence, entrusting her with some of his deepest fears and longings. She, in turn, did the same. And over time, their relationship evolved into a friendship of two peers.

Obviously, it was not an arrangement either of them had ever imagined. At the time of his accident, Brian was only a couple of years removed from leaving home to go off to college. Barbara, on the other hand, was enjoying her newfound freedom as a single woman after years of confinement in an unhappy marriage. But the accident shattered those plans and threw them together again in an unnatural alliance. Brian had nowhere else to turn except to Barbara, and Barbara could not imagine it any other way.

It was a predicament booby-trapped with potential relational landmines. A living arrangement born of necessity rather than choice left its two inhabitants with nowhere to hide. The companionship of one another morning and night was a perpetual reminder of the life each had been forced to renounce. Their mutual disappointment could have easily erupted in a cascade of backbiting and quarreling. That bitterness established no beachhead in their home is a tribute to their resolve. Barbara and Brian might bicker, and they regularly did, but they also appreciated that it was imperative to let it go.

To relieve the tension, they turned to humor. Visitors reported that the walls of the Baco home often reverberated with laughter. Mother and son engaged in a kind of good-natured verbal sparring that was pure Brian Baco. When Barbara grew weary of sitting in the hot summer sun, which he seemed to do endlessly, she chided him, saying, "You'll probably be the only quad to die of skin cancer."

Their banter was infectious. One Saturday afternoon, David and Mike came to visit Brian. As was their ritual, the three buddies blistered each other with a steady diet of wisecracks reminiscent of the chatter one hears in a high school locker room. At one point, Brian sarcastically rebuked his friend, asking, "Mike, have you ever been slapped by a quadriplegic?"

There was about this boy, especially before his injury, an indefatigable love of life. People were enchanted by the easy, self-assured manner with which he carried himself. His quick wit earned him a reputation in school as a class clown. Not satisfied to simply razz his friends, he often turned the jokes on himself in a self-effacing manner that suggested he did not take anything, especially himself, too seriously. His nature was impressively non-neurotic. It was fun being with Brian Baco because Brian Baco had so much fun being with himself. Whether it was spraying Bill Geen's car with a fire extinguisher or setting off a bottle rocket in Dean's bedroom or stealing road signs and leaving them in the yard of a classmate, his commitment to having fun was sure to place him at the center of the action.

Brian's internal battery regularly recharged itself in the company of people. He was energized by discussions about current events, which he approached with his patented skepticism. He was especially suspicious of institutions such as the church, which may explain why he came to identify himself as an atheist. While willing to talk about virtually anything, he clearly adored philosophical discussions on topics such as the existence of God or the merits of cryogenics.

But the harshness of living as a quadriplegic wore some of the luster from Brian's natural exuberance. At times, he was still capable of the old playfulness, but the paralysis, coupled with the ever-present respirator, undermined his previous sense of happy invincibility. At an unnaturally young age, he was forced to confront tough questions about human existence. The unexpected encounter with his mortality accelerated his maturing well beyond that of his peers. He grew impatient with people, especially his own brother, who he observed indulging in mindless, self-destructive behaviors. It seemed incomprehensible to him that people would "waste their lives" when, instead, they could be chasing their dreams.

Barbara describes Brian's broken neck as the line of demarcation marking his metamorphosis: "The first Brian died, and the other Brian arose from that. . .he changed. He took what he had left out of his first life and dealt with it the best he could after the initial getting over and accepting what happened, which was not an easy thing for him to accept. But once he accepted it and decided to live until he died, he was different; he was not the same. I loved him no less than I did before, but it was a different Brian."

Brian frequently used the expression "before I got hurt" to distinguish between his pre- and post-injury self. The old Brian lived for excitement while the resurrected version could only look at the precious opportunity he had squandered and label it "stupid."

A kind person at heart, his sensitivity about the suffering of others grew finer after his accident. Linda Ashley, a family friend, tells of an occasion when she was personally touched by his thoughtfulness. Linda's son, Joey, had led a troubled life that included substance abuse and prison time for a conviction as a drug courier. After his girlfriend ended their relationship, a despondent Joey, convinced he had nothing more to live for, shot and killed himself. A devastated Linda traveled to Florida to attend her son's funeral. Her return home to South Carolina a week later was greeted by phone calls, notes, and flowers from well-wishers. Yet none surprised her more than the call she received that first weekend at home from Brian expressing his condolences and asking if he might come to visit her immediately. She agreed to see him that same weekend.

Despite the difficulties inherent in such a trip, Barbara sensed that it was important to him and agreed to make the 90-minute drive to Linda's home south of Charlotte, North Carolina. But after arriving there, they discovered Linda's house was inaccessible to Brian's wheelchair. Since the weather that day was pleasant, they decided to move the meeting to the backyard beneath a shady tree. Over lunch, Brian explained his reason for coming to see her.

"I wanted to tell you again that I was sorry to hear about Joey," he said.

"Thank you, Brian," she said, her voice beginning to crack. "I just wish I could have been there and done something to stop him. He had his problems, but he was a good boy at heart."

"I know you feel bad, real bad, right now," he said, measuring his words. "But don't give up, Linda. It's going to get better. It just takes time."

Their encounter that day left Linda deeply affected. She can still close her eyes and see Brian strapped into his wheelchair on that breezy afternoon pleading with her to keep on living. She was astonished both by the courage and presence this young man displayed in voluntarily taking on such an assignment many adults would have avoided. She was equally moved by his capacity to step outside his own misery to console her. Perhaps because of his own experience, Brian appreciated that when people find themselves lost, what they need most are friends generous and courageous enough to seek them out.

Chapter 18

One of the most intriguing things about Barbara and Brian's relationship was the contrast in their personalities. Where Brian was cool and rational in his approach to life, Barbara tends to be more impulsive and intuitive. Yet one of the genuine strengths of their union was a remarkable capacity for accepting their respective differences.

Barbara often grumbled about his obsession with the computer and how it interfered with her household duties, just as Brian complained about having to abide the incessant barking of her dogs in the backyard and a cat named Zack that had an unwelcome habit of climbing into bed with him. Yet at the end of the day, the two of them were simpatico.

When Brian watched sports on television, Barbara sometimes curled up beside him for a nap. When conflict arose over his fondness for sitting in the sun and her preference for shade, she purchased a baby monitor that allowed her to remain indoors where it was cool. They discovered ways to make their differences work, without either person feeling diminished.

This commitment to the relationship produced a bond that was stronger than what either of them was likely to manage alone. When Barbara got swept up in the powerful current of her emotions and was poised to respond impulsively, she could count on Brian for calm analysis of a situation. Likewise, friends observed how he gradually learned to express his feelings, a development they attribute to Barbara's influence.

On the surface, it appeared to be a living arrangement where a disabled person was entirely dependent upon another who was able-bodied. But that appearance belies the realities of their life together. There is no doubt that Brian relied heavily upon his mother for his physical survival. Barbara faithfully attended to every last detail of his care. He was indebted to her on one hand, but troubled by it on the other. He fretted over what he perceived to be a serious imbalance in their relationship that left him feeling helpless. Yet as the layers of their living arrangement are peeled away, what remains is a human relationship that was infinitely more complex.

True, Barbara was extended to the point of exhaustion by the demands of caring for Brian, but, at the same time, her sacrifices did not go uncompensated. In her elder son, she discovered a companionship and a sense of belonging for which she as an adopted child had been searching her whole life. She still refers to Brian as her "teacher," implying that it was she who was beholden to him. The fact is, when Barbara was not taking care of her son, he was taking care of her. She discussed everything with him—work, relationships, fears, disappointments. She longed to know what he thought about it all. No one else's opinion mattered nearly as much.

As much as they appreciated company, many times the two of them were perfectly content to be alone with each other. They spoke endlessly about things petty and important, lighthearted and serious, and it was the vitality of those exchanges that sustained them. Barbara considers it good fortune that the person to whom she was so closely bound turned out to be Brian.

"If this had happened with Dean, it would have been hell," she admits. "Dean and I would have had nothing in common to have this bond."

The risk, though, is to romanticize the relationship so as to understate its challenges. Prior to the accident, Brian was an affable, pleasant kid, who except for his late night carousing with friends, generally behaved without malice or guile.

However, the injury to his spine created extraordinary stress in his life and intensified the dark side of his personality. A compulsive streak ran through him, and perhaps more than any other single trait was responsible for his many accomplishments. Whether the task was academics or athletics, he drove himself relentlessly to excel. But this same tendency, manifesting itself in a rigid, stubborn streak, could exasperate his caregivers.

After years of staying awake until Brian was ready to sleep, Barbara finally purchased a timer for the television that switched it off automatically at a preset time. But if the timer turned off the television even a minute too soon, there was hell to pay. If the television in her room was too loud, Brian would yell at her to turn it down. If she, on the other hand, wanted to stay up past his bedtime, he became easily annoyed by the noise. There was an unspoken expectation that the end of her day should coincide with his.

Brian also demanded punctuality from his mother, grumbling when she was even a few minutes late returning home from work. Beginning with his stay at Shepherd Spinal Center, silence was expected in the house between the hours of 10 and 11 so as not to disturb his nightly viewing of *Star Trek* episodes. Often too exhausted to resist, Barbara found herself backpedaling in clashes with her son, acquiescing even when she knew that his demands were contrary to his best interest.

"You always did things the way Brian wanted," she says.

It is not difficult to imagine that a young man whose world had been shattered would try to compensate for it by a rigid need to control what remained. He found reassurance in a regular, reliable schedule and brooded when changes were introduced that upset his daily routine.

Nowhere was Brian's fastidious nature more evident than in his eating habits. He preferred, for example, that the different items on his plate not overlap, causing Barbara to contemplate only half in jest the idea of substituting institutional trays for her traditional dinnerware. Brian was equally particular about who fed him, entrusting that responsibility only to his mother and later his nurses, Ruby Craig and Deborah Seay. Each became thoroughly versed in the size of the portions to serve him, the pace at which to serve each bite, and even the combinations of food he preferred. For others, though, that duty was strictly off limits. At times, Barbara would feed her son breakfast before leaving for work, and nothing more would touch his lips until she returned home that evening.

One Thanksgiving, Barbara spent most of the day in the kitchen preparing the traditional turkey dinner. A family friend, who was a guest for the holiday, volunteered to feed Brian to allow Barbara the rare pleasure of enjoying her own food while it was still warm.

After the guest left, Barbara could tell by his silence that Brian was angry with her.

"Okay, Brian, what is it? What did I do this time?" she asked irritably.

"You know I don't like anybody feeding me," he snapped. "Why did you let her do it?"

"I don't know, maybe I just decided to do something for myself for a change."

"Well, in the future, if you can't feed me yourself, just don't bother."

There it was spelled out in its plain, unvarnished form—the law according to Brian Baco. It was a law based on the realization that eating is one of the most personal of all human acts, every bit as intimate as grooming or going to the bathroom.

For Barbara, there was always that limbo of unresolved ambivalence. Loving Brian dearly, she nevertheless resented the imposition of his disability. From the night he was injured, her orbit became perpetually fixed around his needs. As a family friend remembers, "[There were] so many days that were identical, all run together. [There was] always the computer, always getting him to bed."

While nurses were present during the day, for much of the time Barbara was, for the most part, the person in charge of keeping Brian alive. She never felt entirely comfortable relinquishing his care to anyone else. She refused to even close the door to her bedroom at night because of the fear it caused her son.

Compounding the difficulty of her life was her own stubborn refusal to take shortcuts. Barbara was determined to provide her son with as much normalcy as quadriplegia would permit. When Brian was out of bed, he was always fully clothed, right down to his socks and shoes. Dressing and undressing a two-hundred-plus-pound paralytic each day was no small feat. It would have been so much easier to leave him in pajamas, but Barbara was adamant—only invalids lounge in pajamas all day. She crawled out of bed before dawn each morning and wrestled clothes onto his uncooperative body in defense of his dignity.

Her defensiveness included a prickly sensitivity whenever she felt Brian was being slighted because of his disability. New nurses would invariably direct questions to her that she curtly redirected to her son, explaining for their benefit that paralysis had not affected his ability to hear or speak for himself. Complicating matters in the beginning were the mother figures hovering about, ready to pounce upon any perceived neediness at the slightest provocation. In time, an unspoken manifesto was enacted in the Baco household, declaring Brian was to be treated with the same respect afforded any other adult. No decisions regarding his person were to be made without first obtaining his permission.

Barbara contends, and those closest to her confirm, that she had very little personal life after the accident. On those rare occasions she did allow herself an outing with friends, the advance planning was so extensive as to leave her wondering if it was worth the trouble. Real relaxation was futile anyway as her attention invariably drifted to thoughts of home. Operating always on Brian Baco standard time, she saw to it that her return home coincided with his nightly care. And even when she was not watching the clock, thoughts for his safety were perpetually in the back of her mind.

Attempts at dating were also futile. She recalls preparing an intimate dinner one evening, replete with candles and soft music. There they were, a romantic little threesome—Barbara, her date, and Brian in his wheelchair. Forced to choose, her heart ultimately belonged to Brian. Of course, Brian's duplicity didn't help her social life either. He encouraged his mother to develop a personal life but resented anyone, including the family dogs, who competed for her attention.

In reality, Barbara had very little energy for dating. Nor could she muster much enthusiasm for keeping house or home decorating, especially with her living room held hostage by a hospital bed.

Family friend Emily Horton was a guest at the Bacos' for a few days, which sharpened her appreciation for Barbara's plight. She observed that whenever Barbara went to take a shower, the baby monitor always accompanied her. Barbara could not do the simplest tasks, including drying her hair or taking out the garbage, without the presence of another responsible person in the house. Then there was the constant wheezing of the respirator, which kept Emily awake all night.

Emily also recalls the time when Barbara agreed to go with her to the beach for a rare weekend away. She first had to secure Herman's commitment to drive up from Florida to sit with Brian. Upon checking into their hotel room on Friday afternoon, Barbara laid down on the bed for a "short nap." When she finally awakened the next morning, it was apparent to Emily that her friend was suffering from acute physical exhaustion. How, Emily asked herself, does one cope with such a relentless state of readiness without losing one's sanity?

Linda Ashley came to a similar conclusion after an experience of sitting with Brian while Barbara ran a short errand. Linda was apprehensive about the assignment, expressing fear that the respirator might stop while Barbara was away. Brian, who reluctantly gave his consent for Linda to watch him, was nervous as well, asking that she place the ambu bag on his chest so that it would be easy to reach in an emergency. Those few minutes of responsibility sharpened Linda's awareness to certain nuances of her friend's life. Besides the anxiety it churned up in her, she was struck by the effect Barbara's short absence had on Brian. She recalls how agitated he became and remained the entire time Barbara was gone. She also remembers seeing him visibly relax only after his mother walked through the door again. As a trained social worker, she appreciated the considerable strain that such dependence must have imposed upon their relationship.

Barbara acknowledges her own shadows with refreshing candor. She speaks freely about the resentment she felt toward Brian at times. There was the obligation of those things she had to do for him regardless of her own feelings. And there was frustration with all she could not do for herself while serving as his primary caregiver.

At the time of the accident, she was a relatively young woman in her early 40s who was just beginning to spread her wings. As much as she adored her son and delighted in his company, she realized that some valuable years of her own life were slipping away, years that could have served as a springboard to a professional career and pursuing an adult relationship. She was left to wonder what might have been. These thoughts were possibly the only things she did not have the heart to share with Brian. How could she tell her son, already tortured by fears he was a burden, that he really was? And if she couldn't tell Brian, with whom could she share such dark thoughts? There was no local support group for parents of quadriplegics. She was left with no choice but to swallow hard and live with it. Loving her son deeply, she still resented his stupid stunt and what it had cost her personally.

There were days, she admits, that leaving work she would say to herself, "I can't go home. I can't go home. I don't want to go home. I don't want to be in this anymore."

Chapter 19

With a brand-new Ford van to chauffeur him back and forth to school, Brian re-enrolled at Dorman High School as a full-time student for his senior year. While welcoming the return to campus life, he dreaded facing his peers. In his own words, he felt like a "freak."

It was a self-consciousness reinforced by the embarrassment of an occasional leaky catheter. There were occasions when he had to be dismissed from class early because the catheter failed, leaving his clothes soaked in his own urine.

The bind for him and those who cared about him was that his deep longing to be treated like everyone else was trumped by a severe disability that necessitated exceptional accommodation. The high school administration and faculty tried to balance his physical needs with sensitivity for his feelings about being singled out. But when those two objectives clashed, as inevitably they did, sensitivity had to give way to practicality.

For instance, class schedules and classroom locations were juggled to ensure Brian's classes were all held on the first floor of the building. Since he was unable to write, teachers either administered him oral exams or allowed him to sit at the back of the room and dictate answers to his nurse.

At first, the return to school created a buzz on campus. His story had become a matter of local lore within the student body. Sightings of Brian motoring around campus in his sip and puff wheelchair drew attention from students unaccustomed to seeing someone so severely disabled. But as the academic year dragged on, the novelty faded, and students became distracted by other interests, for which Brian was relieved.

The return to campus restored some normalcy to his daily routine and renewed his association with classmates he had not seen in two years. It also provided the setting of the one and only time he would fall in love.

For all the history Barbara and Brian had together and for all they had come to mean to one another, their mutual devotion would be supremely tested by an unexpected arrival. Sisters Leslie and Abby Smith, the Bacos' neighbors on Runnymeade Drive, were also Brian's friends, and following his accident, they fell into a habit of walking down the street to visit him.

Then one afternoon, the sisters were joined by Elizabeth Balaram, their pretty, petite, dark-haired friend. The intelligent and athletic girl was almost painfully shy, yet Brian liked her immediately. He admired the way she looked and when on those rare occasions she did speak, he appreciated what she had to say. He was especially flattered that she seemed to be attracted to him.

But their introduction was hardly a chance encounter. Elizabeth had long been aware of Brian Baco. She first spotted him after school a couple of years earlier during a workout on the school track. She was immediately attracted to the young athlete as she watched him practice nearby with the school soccer team. However, that initial attraction turned to disappointment when she later learned that he was dating another girl on her track team. By the following fall, Brian had moved with his father to Pensacola, and Elizabeth resigned herself to the fact she was unlikely to ever lay eyes on him again.

Then came Brian's accident and his return to Spartanburg. Elizabeth, who was a junior at Dorman at the time, discovered that her friend Leslie knew him, and her interest in Brian was renewed. She asked Leslie to arrange an introduction.

The chemistry between the two of them was immediate. Elizabeth's visits to the Baco home soon increased in frequency and duration.

Finally, in a move that was downright forward for such a bashful girl, she began to call on Brian without the Smith sisters, a development that raised no objections from him.

At first, they cautiously labeled their mutual attraction a friendship. But after spending a week apart while Elizabeth was out of town, their reunion included acknowledgement that their feelings were much more than platonic.

Brian was quite naturally overcome. He was courted by a girl who could clearly see his impairment but was strangely undeterred by it. And there was no denying Elizabeth's intention to have Brian despite the strong objection of more reasonable voices.

Mike Burnette recalls Elizabeth as an attractive but otherwise unremarkable girl. He believes that under more normal circumstances Brian might have dated her for a short time before eventually losing interest. But, of course, the circumstances of Brian's life were far from normal. Inexperienced in love, but no fool, he realized this was perhaps his only chance at a relationship with a girl, and he was not about to discourage her. Like all new lovers, he fawned over Elizabeth when she was present and brooded in her absences.

At the time of their introduction, Elizabeth's home life was in a state of disintegration. She was as desperate to grow up as her parents were to hang on, resulting in messy confrontations and alienation. The romantic relationship she began to develop with Brian took the family's problems to a new level of unhappiness. From the outset, the Balarams objected to their daughter's interest in a boy whose disability, they were convinced, offered her no future. But the more vigorous their objections and the harder they worked to keep the young couple apart, the more determined Elizabeth was to have Brian in her life.

While the Balarams resisted, Barbara supported or at least tolerated the budding romance. She provided transportation and resources for their evenings out. But most of all, she kept a low profile so that Brian and Elizabeth had the necessary space to cultivate their relationship. Their dates, unremarkable by teen standards, consisted mostly of movies and eating out. But given the difficulty of transporting Brian anywhere, they were just as content to remain at the house playing computer games, watching television, or simply sitting outside on the deck listening to music. It really made little difference so long as they were together.

In contrast to the reaction of the Balarams, the adults in Brian's life took delight in this development. Although it was plain to see the relationship was not likely to last, there was no ignoring how Brian's eyes sparkled whenever Elizabeth entered the room nor could they deny their immense gratitude for the lovely diversion she represented. It was in the privacy of his own home that Brian wooed Elizabeth. With his hands unavailable to caress her, he instead turned up the jets on the old Brian Baco charm. Years later, Elizabeth can still recall the irresistibility of his gentleness, the patience and intensity with which he listened to her, and his knack for always saying just the right thing. With her own family life in chaos, she sought and found sanctuary at Brian's side. Where her parents seemed intent on imposing their will, he expressed appreciation for hers. Where they lectured, Brian listened. Where they scolded, Brian made her laugh. It was no contest, really. Elizabeth's parents drove her to Brian, ensuring the very outcome they most dreaded.

Temperamentally, the young lovers appeared to complement one another well. Brian relied on his keen sense of humor and conversational skills to draw the reserved Elizabeth out of her shell. By this time, he was adept at the role of comforting a disconsolate woman, having provided that same service to his mother.

Elizabeth reciprocated by standing faithfully by his bed or perched on the edge of it gazing adoringly at him. Her devotion soothed the ache in Brian to be treated as a normal person. Here, standing at his side each day was a girl who voluntarily chose him as her companion. Unlike his mother or his friends, she shared no history with him and was under no obligation to him. She could have cut and run at any time. Instead, she remained steadfastly at his side, reassuring him with kisses and the gentle strokes of her fingertips across his face, partially restoring Brian's sense of manhood.

When asked how she coped with the fact that Brian could not touch her, Elizabeth grows defensive and rebuts the question by pointing out that no one ever "touched" her in the way he did. For a young girl wounded by domestic conflict, his acceptance proved to be the ultimate seduction, sweeping her up in a euphoria that no physical pleasure could equal. The spell he managed to cast over her without being able to lift a single finger was pure intoxicant.

Chapter 20

Meanwhile, Denny Webb was proceeding with work on the Baco family lawsuit against Dr. Calvert McCorkle. After a series of delays, the trial was finally set for the spring of 1988.

Denny sought and was granted a change of venue. He also succeeded in establishing Florida as Brian's legal residence at the time of the accident. Since the lawsuit involved parties from two different states and the damages sought exceeded $10,000, the case fell under federal jurisdiction, and the trial was scheduled for the nearest federal district courthouse located in Greenville, just thirty miles from Spartanburg. Denny was relieved to have the trial moved out of McCorkle's "backyard," because Spartanburg was a small, conservative town, where attacks upon a prominent local surgeon were likely to be looked upon with disfavor, especially when the salvos were fired at him by an out-of-town, big city lawyer. And while Greenville was hardly a cosmopolitan alternative, the fact it was not Spartanburg counted as a victory for the plaintiff.

Months prior to the trial date, both sides prepared a list of witnesses and began the tedious process of deposing them. Depositions are the legal means by which attorneys collect facts in a case to begin to construct a courtroom strategy. Once a witness' story is established in a deposition, their testimony can be challenged later during the trial.

Despite the strength of his convictions, Denny was not naïve about the prospects for this case. It is one thing to defend a client against charges of malpractice; it is another thing altogether to convince a jury someone is guilty of it. The burden in civil cases is with the plaintiff, who must persuade an entire jury that there is a preponderance of evidence pointing to "professional negligence." Finding McCorkle liable for damages would require a unanimous vote of all eight jurors.

Furthermore, Denny understood he would have to overcome the natural deference the jury of lay people was likely to extend to a doctor. Although the pattern is gradually changing, historically, a lawyer rarely defeats a doctor in a medical malpractice suit in South Carolina. Physicians, like clergy, are still revered in the Deep South. Juries, especially unsophisticated ones, are predisposed to believe doctors are immune to incompetence or malfeasance. The playing field is further skewed by the reputation of attorneys themselves, who are sometimes perceived as preying upon a defendant for their own personal gain.

However, Denny's personal opinion of the medical profession is not nearly so flattering as that of juries. After devoting much of his career to the defense of doctors, he characterizes many of them as "prima donnas" who call "day and night." He complains that doctors "don't like attorneys until they need us. They are your best friend if they do."

But the obstacles he faced in trying this case were more substantial than the bad blood that exists between the two professions. For one thing, all of the NICU nurses were prepared to corroborate McCorkle's account of the story. When a nurse as experienced and reliable as Kathy Johnson took the witness stand to testify Brian's shoulder shrugs were weakening prior to the surgery, it lent even greater credibility to the doctor's case.

Denny interpreted the nurses' corroboration as capitulation to an authority figure. Since public contradiction of a superior's word could be occupational suicide, he believed the nurses had no choice but to back McCorkle.

While politics cannot be dismissed as a factor, the truth is probably more complex. The neurosurgeon in question had a shared history with this nursing staff. From many years of assisting him in his practice, they were intimately acquainted with his aggressive approach to spinal cord injuries and were not likely to find anything inconsistent about either his handling of Brian's case or his incomplete progress notes.

As Kathy pointed out, the NICU had been successful based on a team-oriented approach that emphasized mutual respect.

In his own deposition, McCorkle acknowledged the degree to which he depended on the nursing staff to monitor and assess the condition of his patients. With one of their own now threatened by a lawsuit, the nurses may have responded with an unambiguous display of solidarity. They also were part of the same medical establishment that feels threatened by the current litigious atmosphere. For nurses, like doctors, can be sued for malpractice.

The result was that Denny could find no member of the medical team to challenge the surgeon's handling of the case. His efforts were further frustrated by the fact that he had no better luck with the local doctors.

The neurosurgeons in Spartanburg and Greenville he contacted either sided with McCorkle or refused to become involved. At the time of the trial, there were less than two dozen neurosurgeons practicing in the entire state of South Carolina. Among other things, it would be socially awkward to challenge a colleague's practices in a courtroom and later encounter him during cocktails at a medical society meeting.

Physicians in general are particularly touchy these days about lawsuits. Some believe they are under siege at the hands of unscrupulous litigators who sue them without cause, driving up the cost of their malpractice insurance. Whether or not their complaints are justified is subject to much debate, but it does seem evident that physicians who agree to give expert testimony against colleagues may feel they are encouraging the filing of lawsuits in general. And the accusatory finger they point in the direction of a colleague today may be turned on them the next time around.

Unable to secure the services of a local neurosurgeon to testify against McCorkle, Denny turned next to Shepherd Spinal Center. There was a promising conversation with a physician at Shepherd who collaborated on Brian's case. But he says the doctor was reluctant to accuse a colleague of malpractice, a matter that was further complicated because McCorkle's practice was a regular source of patient referrals to Shepherd.

Denny painstakingly negotiated with the anxious doctor over specific language that could be used other than malpractice to describe McCorkle's management of the case. However, during his subsequent deposition, the doctor declined to say for the public record what he had agreed to in private.

Denny did manage to locate one Atlanta neurosurgeon who was willing to testify about McCorkle's supposed negligence. But by this time, the doctor was in his 80s and had a reputation for unpredictable behavior. In his conversations with Denny, he displayed flashes of brilliant commentary interspersed with remarks that were bizarre, bordering on nonsensical. Denny ultimately determined the man was a "loose cannon," and abandoned plans to call him as a witness.

As a last resort, Denny turned once more to Dr. Udvarhelji for help. Affiliated at the time with the Technical Advisory Service for Attorneys, Udvarhelji was familiar with litigation, having reviewed medical records, according to his own recollection, in approximately thirty cases and testified in several as an expert witness. His retired status insulated him against professional retaliation, and the fact he no longer had a career to protect gave him license to speak publicly with candor.

But his services did not come cheap. His fee was $200 per hour for depositions and $2,000 per day, plus expenses, for trials. For his money, Denny hoped the retired neurosurgeon's vast experience in the field, coupled with his impressive pedigree, would lend added credibility to the case he was building.

Yet along with his assets, Denny's money was also purchasing Udvarhelji's rather conspicuous liabilities. He was an outsider both because he lived in Baltimore and because of the thickness of his foreign accent. His exotic heritage combined with the disclosure that he was a "hired gun" imported expressly for the trial and paid a hefty fee for his services was not likely to sit well with a jury of local people.

In contrast, McCorkle's star witness was Greenville neurosurgeon Dr. Frank Wrenn, widely regarded not only for his professional accomplishments but also because of his service to the community. Unlike Udvarhelji, Wrenn received no compensation for his testimony, which added further gravity to his opinion.

Another factor complicating the case was the challenge of communicating highly technical information about spinal cord injuries. Not only would Denny be called upon to explain complex medical conditions like subluxation and edema, he would have to do so in language understandable to the jury. The struggle for clarity was a kind of pressure not shared by his counterpart in the courtroom. Since the defense attorney's task was to deflect an attack rather than prove an accusation, the obscurity of medical references was an asset rather than a liability.

There was one other inarguable fact working against Denny in this case: Brian Baco had clearly visited this misfortune upon himself. The night of the accident he violated a series of laws that included consumption of alcohol as a minor and trespassing on and vandalizing private property. There was no denying that Brian had been crippled neither by a tragic accident nor some wretched disease, but as a result of his own reckless behavior. McCorkle may or may not have been negligent in his handling of the case, but Brian was clearly the chief perpetrator of his own misery. Denny might work to mitigate the impact of that knowledge at the trial, but he could never entirely erase it from the minds of those eight jurors.

The defendant was deposed twice in preparation for the trial. Nothing in Denny's previous experience with physicians had prepared him for the likes of Calvert McCorkle. He has come to think of neurosurgeons as the special forces of the medical profession: specialists who generally "look like doctors on soap operas."

Members of a high-risk, high-reward specialty, their hefty liability insurance premiums tend to match the size of their egos. Denny describes these virtuosos of the medical community as bright, accomplished, and polished individuals who are motivated by the exceptional, sometimes impossible, challenges of their specialty.

But he found McCorkle's image defied that stereotype. During the depositions, the neurosurgeon often spoke in disjointed, rambling sentences. His testimony included some inconsistencies and misstatements that an accomplished professional would be expected to easily sidestep.

For example, he first justified Brian's surgery as a means of slowing the deterioration of his condition, only later to contradict himself in another statement where he explained that surgery would only stabilize the spine, not slow the deterioration. At one point, he acknowledged having treated other patients whose paralysis had ascended, but later reversed himself by claiming Brian was his first ascension case ever. He spoke confidently of the importance of quickly moving his patient to Shepherd for rehabilitation, but admitted he wasn't exactly sure what rehabilitation would do for him. He boasted that at the time in question he had nine other patients in the hospital "all as sick as Brian." Ten neuro patients would have swamped the available resources in a community as small as Spartanburg. What's more, Brian was injured, not "sick," as the doctor suggested.

Perhaps McCorkle's ineffective performance in the depositions can be attributed to a case of nerves. He surely had much at stake professionally. Malpractice lawsuits are anathema to doctors as scandals are to politicians. There was the potential public embarrassment should he lose the case compounded by peripheral damage to his professional reputation.

Despite Denny's unflattering assessment of the man, McCorkle did indeed possess a neurosurgeon's pedigree. He was selected chief resident in the final year of his residency, passed his board examination on the first try, and was established in his own practice before his 32nd birthday. After graduating as part of the 1972 class at the Medical University of South Carolina, he accepted a general surgery internship at the North Carolina Baptist Hospital and the Bowman Gray School of Medicine in Winston-Salem, North Carolina, followed by a five-year residency in neurosurgery at George Washington Medical Center. After completing his training, he moved to Spartanburg in 1979 where he began a partnership with Robert Flandry and Darwin Keller.

Neurosurgery is an intensely stressful occupation. Its practitioners are confronted each day with gravely ill and injured patients who often suffer from life-threatening conditions. These patients are victims of brain tumors, blood clots, auto accidents, and gunshot wounds. Permanent disability is not unusual, nor is death. Neurosurgeons are expected to treat injuries and diseases of the central nervous system that include processes so minute they are mostly invisible to the naked eye. As McCorkle stated in his deposition, performing operations on the brain, spine, and peripheral nerves could take up to 18 hours. The work is tedious yet extremely delicate, often carried out under the lens of a microscopic camera. It calls for exceptional concentration and an ability to perform well under stressful conditions.

While Brian's injury would seem extraordinary to the average person, McCorkle characterized the case as "an everyday occurrence" in his practice.

Chapter 21

By the time federal judge Joe Anderson gaveled the court into session on April 25, 1988, nearly two years had passed since Brian's accident. Denny Webb's own involvement in the case now spanned eighteen months. He and his staff had invested hundreds of hours pursuing witnesses, tracking down leads, and taking depositions for which his law firm had not been paid a single cent.

In the days before the trial, he began to organize his material in a process he compares to "preparing for war." He contends that effective litigators must possess clear and persuasive speaking skills but also demonstrate the mental agility to improvise when a trial takes some unexpected turn, as it invariably will.

Since it is impossible to anticipate exactly how courtroom proceedings will unfold, litigators also must have exceptional powers of concentration and stamina. Denny recalls retiring bone-weary to his hotel room at the end of each day but with preparation for the next day still looming before him. Yet it is this very challenge of actually trying a case that keeps him fascinated with his profession. A lawsuit alleging malpractice is often played for high stakes that include large sums of money, professional reputations, and big egos. Among its most damaging potential consequences are the public insinuations about the competence of the individual being sued. Such personal attacks have the capacity to pierce right to the soft, vulnerable core of a human being. Clients who are understandably anxious about the outcome pay Denny handsomely, expecting that he will succeed in insulating them from further embarrassment and vindicate their reputations. Thus the opening day of a trial, as Denny describes it, is a schizophrenic adrenaline rush, alternating between exhilaration about trying the case and the dread of losing it.

However, the stress he experienced as he prepared to represent the Baco family was of a different kind. Because the client was not compensating him for his services, there was no pressure for his courtroom performance to justify his fee. Nor was he counting on the case to generate more clients for his firm. Instead, he badly wanted to win a settlement for the Bacos because he appreciated the depth of the family's predicament.

Throughout the trial, Denny held Dave in his mind as a reminder of all a person with a C-5 level spinal cord injury was capable of accomplishing. There was Dave's marriage and his career, of course, but also the assortment of ordinary tasks he learned anew that when taken as a whole helped to restore his dignity as a functional human being. Whether writing his name, feeding himself, or brushing his teeth, with every reclaimed skill, Denny saw his brother's quality of life enriched.

He remembers the day Dave settled behind the steering wheel of his specially equipped bread truck for the first time. It was the single most important occasion of Dave's entire disability. With his own wheels, Dave had achieved real independence in a culture where driving an automobile is a cherished privilege.

The memory of his brother thriving despite his handicap provided the yardstick against which Denny measured Brian Baco's prospects. Dave was what Brian might have become without the ascension, and likewise, Dave was what Brian would never become because of it. It was the degree of devastation facing the boy and his family that was to inform Denny's performance in the courtroom that week.

As the case went to trial, Brian was twenty-two months deep into his adjustment to living with quadriplegia. The following fall he was planning to enroll in the University of South Carolina at Spartanburg (USCS), where he had been accepted as an undergraduate. Despite the limitations imposed by paralysis and the awkwardness of the respirator, his plans remained ambitious. A sizable settlement from the lawsuit would help to underwrite the pursuit of his long-term objectives for a career and a family.

Because Brian was still a minor, his father was appointed as his guardian ad litem, and the lawsuit was filed in Herman's name. The official complaint brought against the defendant alleged that the plaintiff "has lost the services and companionship of his sixteen-year-old son." The preliminary activities that first day joined McCorkle's partner at Spartanburg Neurological Associates, Darwin Keller, as a defendant in the case, signifying that the lawsuit was being brought against the partnership. Witnesses in the trial were banned from the courtroom until their scheduled appearance to prevent possible complicity in their testimony. The jury, consisting of five men and three women, was seated and sworn in, and opening statements were presented by Denny and his counterpart, Greenville attorney Dewey Oxner.

There are no actual transcripts of the proceedings, as they are not ordinarily filed in civil cases where there is no appeal. But from interviews with some of the participants and examination of the depositions that have been preserved at the Federal Records Center in Atlanta, a rough outline of what occurred that week in court can be pieced together.

After studying the medical records and deposing dozens of witnesses, Denny, with Dr. Udvarhelji's help, organized his case by identifying for the jurors six specific occasions when he believed the doctor was guilty of negligence. According to Denny, McCorkle failed to properly immobilize Brian's neck; failed to perform the necessary diagnostic tests to determine the extent of the spinal damage; failed to document examination of the patient at prescribed intervals; performed surgery prematurely; used an inappropriate surgical procedure that caused further damage to the spine; and failed to correct his work after X-rays taken in the recovery room revealed the broken bone was still not properly aligned.

Barbara, Brian's maternal grandmother, younger brother Dean, and family friend Jan Brown all testified that they had witnessed the patient raising his left arm to his chest in the emergency room the night of the accident. Jan also recalled that Brian had applied pressure when she grasped his hand during their visit that night. Rehabilitation specialists testified about quality of life and economic issues for quadriplegics. And Denny established how Brian's quality of life deteriorated following the ascension of his injury from the C-5 to the C-2 level. Nurses and doctors who worked on the case were challenged on alleged inconsistencies between their deposed statements and the hospital records. Even McCorkle was called to testify.

But the most provocative witness of all may have been Udvarhelji, who challenged virtually every facet of McCorkle's management of the case before, during, and after the surgery. He was critical of McCorkle for everything, from not ordering a CAT scan, to the type of fusion procedure he chose, to the way the spine was immobilized. However, some of these criticisms may have had more to do with individual preference than substance. According to research, there is no one correct way to treat spinal cord injuries. Some specialists administer steroids to reduce swelling; some don't. Some use wire to secure the splint to the broken bone; some don't. Treatment options by a single neurosurgeon may also vary from case to case, depending on the patient and the extent of the injury.

But the thrust of Udvarhelji's dissatisfaction with McCorkle seemed to have as much to do with temperament as technique. He explained that the procedure he taught his students emphasized the use of traction to simultaneously realign the broken bone and immobilize the injury. McCorkle placed Brian in traction at first, but it was after the alignment of the broken bone that the two physicians differed in approach.

McCorkle moved relatively quickly to perform the invasive procedure, operating on his patient just two and a half days after the accident occurred. It was a decision that Udvarhelji challenged in his deposition:

"I would like to repeat that surgery is dangerous in this situation. There's no need for it. I come back again to the statement of leaving him in traction; it can be done [in] a week or so without major danger;

halo, plaster jacket, many ways that [are] not surgery. I would like to make the point that surgery in the acute stage quite often is adding insult to injury. . ."

His own treatment plan called for leaving the patient in traction, frequently evaluating the status of the injured tissue, and performing more sophisticated diagnostic tests before making a decision about surgery. In his opinion, the surgeon's rush to operate contributed to the deterioration of Brian's condition.

Chapter 22

The defense called expert witnesses to contradict Udvarhelji's charge that McCorkle had deviated from standard care. In his deposition, McCorkle characterized his objective as "to get the patient up and get him going." Early transfer to a rehab center is believed to be beneficial to both a patient's physical and mental condition, while lengthy immobilization in a hospital bed can contribute to an assortment of complications to the heart, lungs, and skin as well as possibly compounding the effects of depression.

Dr. Frank Wrenn confirmed that his colleague's treatment plan was consistent with how he would have managed an injury of this severity. Although it was ordinarily his practice to wait at least five days to operate, he acknowledged that he did not consider it inappropriate to perform surgery less than three days after an accident.

Wrenn also expressed reservations about Udvarhelji's strategy of depending solely on a bracing device to stabilize the injured area. He backed his argument by citing a statistic that nationally five percent of all patients with spinal cord injuries will experience some deterioration of their condition irrespective of the type of treatment they receive, a figure that includes those patients who receive no surgery at all. In his professional opinion, Brian was a victim of random statistical misfortune rather than a physician's negligence.

Wrenn helped establish the defense's position that Dr. Udvarhelji's testimony constituted an opinion. And Udvarhelji's hefty $2,000 per day fee gave him plenty of inspiration for assuming the role of a skeptic.

Still, the retired neurosurgeon's observations do offer a contrasting approach to conventional medical practices here in the West. McCorkle is a surgeon, a highly trained body mechanic, whose livelihood depends on assessing damage and making necessary repairs. His bias is toward surgery. He admitted in his deposition that he was "always thinking about surgery," a fact confirmed by the progress notes in which he scribbled "will plan surgery" just hours after taking the case.

In his deposition, Udvarhelji argued for a more cautious model of medicine, referring to what has been learned about the potential danger of surgery as a treatment for a condition of the brain called intracerebral hematomas: "We operated for years with terrible results. Now we have the CAT scan, and we can see that nature helps these patients, and they do recover, and we don't add an injury, and they are better off, so the basic principle is a more conservative approach. . .let nature occasionally help us."

Udvarhelji was appealing for greater restraint in the treatment of a spinal cord injury. It wasn't that he opposed surgery. Rather, he believed that by waiting seven to ten days, a window of opportunity was introduced for the body to unleash its own natural healing powers. The interim also allowed time for the spinal shock to subside and to gather more information about the extent of the injury before proceeding with a risky invasive procedure.

He was also critical of McCorkle for what he interpreted as inattention. His own stated preference called for regular examination of the patient at four-, six-, or eight-hour intervals. In Brian's case, there is nothing in the medical record to indicate examinations took place at such intervals throughout the day. What notes do exist are sketchy and illegibly scrawled in the style of a busy man in an enormous hurry. Those same notes reveal that McCorkle had reached a diagnosis and treatment plan within hours of first examining the patient, a plan from which he showed no intention of deviating.

McCorkle stated during his deposition that Brian's condition was deteriorating prior to surgery. No supporting documentation of this exists anywhere in the progress notes. His discharge summary does describe a pre-operative weakening of his biceps function and shoulder shrugs, but that document was dictated more than two weeks *after*

Brian's discharge from the hospital.

In his first deposition, McCorkle claimed Brian showed signs of respiratory problems as well as lost sensation and motor function prior to surgery, but again there is no evidence of this in the notes. He also recalled a conversation with his associate, Dr. Flandry, in which they discussed their patient's decline before the operation, yet as before, that conversation failed to find its way into the medical records of the case.

Denny found the scarcity of documentation suspicious. He explained to jurors during the trial that one purpose of charting is to preserve a written record of a patient's condition as a means of measuring progress toward recovery.

Curiously, however, the deterioration of Brian's condition after surgery is liberally noted in the medical records. There are numerous references to his loss of respiration, motor function, and sensation post-operatively. On this basis, Denny concluded there had been no deterioration in his client's condition prior to surgery. The evidence, he says, points to the operation itself as the trigger for the ascension of Brian's paralysis.

When challenged on his charting practices during the deposition, McCorkle replied:

". . .we have a very, very busy practice, okay? We have nine people just as sick as Brian and sometimes, you know, every little point, it's difficult, and they get overlooked when trying to write it. Our practice is to try to take care of the patient instead of worrying about all these malpractice suits, but unfortunately when you have nine sick patients as sick as Brian, it's very possible some of the notes were missed that day, but he was seen, it's documented."

Thus, McCorkle's explanation for failing to keep his progress notes current and thorough was predicated on being overworked. And as the doctor himself suggested, accurate charting is mostly a way of protecting one's backside from lawsuits, a practice to be distinguished from trying "to take care of the patient." Yet, one might ask, what is the practice of medicine if not the careful, methodical monitoring and measuring of a patient's progress? And who can ultimately have confidence in a physician who considers losses of sensation, movement, and respiration from a spinal cord injury a "little point" that can be overlooked in his notes? The nurses' progress notes offer a detailed accounting of Brian's eight-day hospitalization; McCorkle's charting practices, on the other hand, tell virtually nothing about his care.

In his deposition, Frank Wrenn acknowledged that charting is important to him personally but that charting practices vary widely in his profession. Having reviewed hospital records from across the country, he reported there is a diversity of styles. It seems some physicians are more disciplined and thorough about their record keeping than others.

When asked in his deposition if performing surgery on Brian two and a half days after his admission to the hospital constituted malpractice, Udvarhelji refused to give a direct answer. He seemed more concerned with McCorkle's perceived failure to complete what he considered the necessary diagnostic studies before deciding on surgery. In the neurosurgeon's discharge summary just two short sentences separate his diagnosis from the prescribed surgical procedure. It was the speed with which he moved from one to the other that Udvarhelji found incomprehensible. Within a few hours of his initial examination, McCorkle had already concluded, irrespective of spinal shock, that the lesion to the spine was total and irreversible.

In his deposition, Wrenn defended his colleague's decision in the following exchange with Denny:

> Q: Do you feel that it is acceptable neurological procedure to make a determination, one, that it's a total cord lesion, and, two, there's nothing neurologically that can be done within three or four hours after the accident?
> A: Yes, I think it's reasonable.
> Q: And you think it's reasonable to do that simply based upon the observations and physical examination of the neurosurgeon but no other tests?

Brian Baco already shows signs of being self-possessed in this photo of him as an infant in Rock Hill, SC.

Dean and Brian pause in one of their calmer moments on Runnymeade Drive.

Brian blows out the candles at the party celebrating his second birthday as Barbara looks on.

Brian as a kindergarten student.

Brian's school picture taken while a student at Woodland Heights Elementary School in Spartanburg.

Brian and Barbara share a moment together on a family outing prior to his diving accident.

Barbara Baco enjoys a day in the North Carolina mountains with sons Dean (center) and Brian.

By junior high school, Brian already dreamed of becoming an aerospace engineer.

Barbara and Brian pause in the garden at Sheperd Spinal Center in Atlanta at the beginning of their sojourn with quadriplegia.

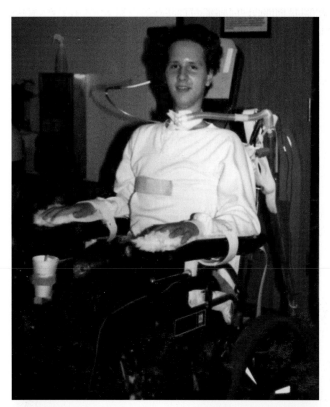

Brian shows off his new Sip and Puff wheelchair.

The Bacos, (L to R) Dean, Herman, Brian, and Barbara, are reunited in this photo taken after Brian returned home from rehabilitation in Atlanta.

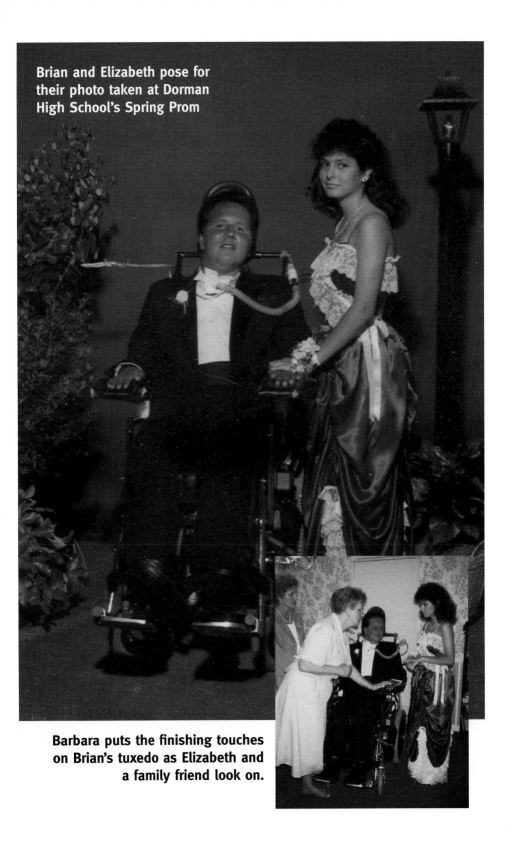

Brian and Elizabeth pose for their photo taken at Dorman High School's Spring Prom

Barbara puts the finishing touches on Brian's tuxedo as Elizabeth and a family friend look on.

Brian served as an honorary groomsman at the wedding of his close friend
Mike Burnette, pictured here with his bride Tracy on their wedding day.

A: I assume you're including—
Q: Except X-rays.
A: I'm assuming you're including that. Yes, I think you can.
Q: Would you?
A: Yes.

Once again reflecting his more cautious approach, Udvarhelji wondered why more sophisticated testing was not done before committing to surgery. In particular, he cited a CAT scan and a myleogram as procedures he would have prescribed to obtain more precise information about the extent of the damaged tissue.

During the deposition, he explained his position in this way: "Deterioration may occur because a free disc fragment is pressing on the cord; deterioration may occur because a free bony chip is pressing on the cord; deterioration may occur because a hematoma developed which is pressing on the cord. . .Deterioration may occur because a cavitation is occurring inside of the cord. . . and that is the reason that you have to pinpoint it."

He also explained that the results of the CAT scan and myleogram would dictate not only whether surgery was necessary but the kind of stabilization procedure to perform. Wrenn countered by saying that such tests were unnecessary and would not likely supply new information.

As the trial wound down, Oxner approached Denny offering to settle the case out of court. His client, who until now had refused to negotiate, agreed to pay $400,000 of the $1 million the Bacos were asking. Appreciating the unpredictability of juries and that this case had considerable "sympathetic" appeal, Oxner admitted there was "a substantial chance of losing the case." With the outcome uncertain, he advised his client to increase the offer to the plaintiff, but McCorkle refused to budge. With his confidence growing in relation to his adversary's newly exposed vulnerability, Denny rejected the offer.

Chapter 23

The jury retired at 12:30 on Friday afternoon and began its deliberations with a straw poll to assess the mood of each of its eight members. A unanimous vote was required to reach a finding either for or against malpractice. While the first polling came up short of a consensus, it was clear that both attorneys had overestimated the strength of the Bacos' case. McCorkle was never seriously in jeopardy of losing the lawsuit during the three hours the jury deliberated. By 3:45, when they returned with their verdict, the group was emotionally spent. They had anguished for most of the afternoon over the irreconcilable interests of the two parties.

As the finding for the defendant Calvert McCorkle was read aloud, a couple of the female jurors began to cry softly. Their male counterparts were no less moved, however. Two men from the jury declined invitations to be interviewed for this book, citing their unwillingness to resurrect unpleasant memories of the past.

Barbara hugged a dejected Denny and told him she was sorry. The gesture seemed to puzzle him. He had had many clients congratulate him over the years for winning their cases but never one to console him after losing.

"It was a fair trial," he says today. "We just lost."

There would be no legal appeal of the verdict, as only courtroom procedures and rulings, not the finding of the jury, can be challenged in a higher court. However, second-guessing the decision to reject the out-of-court settlement was inevitable. After paying the attorney's fee, the Bacos would have realized about a quarter of a million dollars from the settlement. Barbara and Herman acknowledge the windfall could have made an immediate difference.

"I wanted Brian to have a house where he could move around in the whole house," says Barbara. "It would have been comfortable. It would have been warm. It would have been especially for Brian. I would have liked some things for Brian to have helped his life be easier."

But the reality is that $250,000 was not nearly enough to offset the long-term financial burden that lay ahead. And in the end, the family adopted a philosophical attitude about the trial's outcome to salve their disappointment. "We didn't have it," Barbara says, "so we didn't lose it."

Denny's recollections of that week in Greenville, separated by many subsequent depositions and trials, have grown fuzzy with time. What remains crystal clear in his mind, though, is the conviction that McCorkle was negligent in his handling of Brian's case, a subject for which he can still muster a surprising amount of passion.

An objective and reasonable evaluation of the existing records might lead to the following conclusions: The verdict the jury reached seems reasonable based upon the evidence at its disposal. While Udvarhelji's commentary is interesting and perhaps even insightful, the jury did not feel it proved liability on the part of the surgeon.

During his deposition, Frank Wrenn quoted a Latin phrase, "ergo post-propter hoc." It was offered in response to a question posed about whether the surgery may have had an adverse effect on Brian's condition: "It could raise that question. But let me tell you, though, that that falls under one of the very common fallacies about human reasoning. It's what the old philosophers call ergo post-[propter] hoc reasoning. And it assumes that since one situation follows an occurrence, that the occurrence is always the cause of the situation, and it's not so."

Ergo post-propter hoc, more commonly known as cause and effect, has informed human reasoning for thousands of years. It has served as the source of conjecture, superstition, religion, science and all manner of human reasoning throughout history. Sometimes cause and effect does apply. The established relationship between two events is clear and indisputable. For example, it is assumed that pregnancy is the result of sexual intercourse.

But as Wrenn rightly points out, two events occurring in sequence may have little or nothing to do with one another. So that what appears to be a simple matter of B following A turns out to be not so simple at all.

Dr. Charles Fogarty, Brian's pulmonary specialist, dismisses the lawsuit against McCorkle as being "without substance." "One-third of these [spinal cord injury] patients get better, one-third get worse, and one-third stay the same," he says. While his statistics may be challenged, his point is worthy of consideration.

Another possible conclusion would argue that McCorkle may have inflicted suffering on his patient and his patient's family without it constituting malpractice. The hospital records, as well as the neurosurgeon's own testimony, suggest a general disregard for the body's own natural healing powers. Jan Brown recalls the doctor's insistence that Brian needed to have surgery to stabilize his condition before he could be transferred to Shepherd Spinal Center. She says it was only later they learned that Shepherd accepts patients who have not been stabilized all the time.

"Get him up and get him going" is the classic mechanic's response to a broken machine. But surgery is not auto repair. It is a radical response to bodily injury or illness—one that seeks to cure an affliction by first assaulting the organism where the affliction is found. It does not seem unreasonable that a decision of this magnitude should have been preceded by extensive testing, examination and numerous consultations with Brian's family both before and afterward. The hospital records, however, do not reflect such thoroughness, nor do they suggest the kind of urgency that was the justification for surgery.

Based on interviews with family members, it is possible that the lawsuit could have been avoided without significant changes to McCorkle's treatment plan. The injury Brian sustained may have been an "everyday occurrence" for McCorkle, but it was catastrophic for Brian and his family. These overwhelming circumstances were made more difficult by a lack of professional attention.

Oxner describes his former client as a "compassionate man," but that is not an opinion shared by Barbara. She says that so long as the surgeon was procuring permission from the parents to perform surgery, he was attentive. But after the operation, when Brian's condition took that frightening turn for the worse and his family desperately needed support and information, McCorkle and his partners were exasperatingly scarce. Barbara and Herman might catch one of them during rounds for a quick question or two, but the doctors volunteered little information.

Jan Brown remembers the partners' body language communicating: "We've got to go," and "I know what's best." The family interpreted this remoteness as a lack of caring.

But no matter what conclusion is reached about the jury's verdict, there is no denying its largely invisible psychological toll. Winning the lawsuit was expected to join an impressive list of personal accomplishments that had come to characterize Brian's short life as a disabled person.

In less than two years since his accident, he was about to graduate with his high school class despite losing an entire academic year, had gained admission to a four-year college, had captivated a beautiful girl's heart, and had become a computer wizard.

With his legend growing in proportion to his exploits, family and friends expected nothing less than triumph in the courtroom. The outcome of the trial was huge disappointment. "Stunning" and "shocking" are words used to describe their feelings at the time. The failed lawsuit would eventually be identified as the first major slip down a steep descent from which Brian would never manage to recover his previous higher ground.

Chapter 24

B rian was not present for the reading of the verdict. After the judge adjourned the courtroom, Denny drove the thirty miles to Spartanburg to inform his client of the outcome. Before he could reach his destination, Herman had already called his son to deliver the bad news. Brian accepted the verdict with his usual equanimity. He reassured Barbara it was okay, that the money really didn't mean anything to him.

In fact, his adolescent thoughts had already turned to the spring prom he was scheduled to attend that very night with Elizabeth. Brian's decision to participate in the event was one he could be forgiven for avoiding, but it speaks again of his longing for normalcy. It also illustrates the extent to which his family and friends were willing to go to help him achieve it. Barbara, Ruby, Sean Cullen, Linda Ashley, and Emily Horton all assembled at the house the evening of the prom. They were determined to make this a special occasion for him. Even Herman remained in town to lend a hand.

The Baco household was abuzz that night with a sense of anticipation seldom seen there. Barbara rented Brian's tuxedo and, with Ruby's help, wrestled to get him into it. She also purchased a pair of black patent shoes for the occasion. (She returned them to the shoe store the next day for a full refund, explaining they had never been worn.) Emily captured all of the evening's preparatory activities on videotape. Herman, accompanied by Sean and his video camera, drove the van that shuttled the couple first to a local restaurant and later to the dance. Careful not to intrude on Brian and Elizabeth's fun, the two men waited patiently outside.

The night received mixed reviews. The adults who took part were thrilled. It was an evening for nostalgia, with lots of pictures taken and tears shed. From a practical perspective, it represented Brian's deepest incursion into the world of the able-bodied, prompting Linda to describe his decision to attend as "gutsy." By agreeing to attend the prom, he was thrusting himself into the spotlight as never before. Where better to call attention to his useless limbs than at a dance? With his classmates throwing their healthy, vigorous bodies around on the dance floor, he was relegated to the sidelines with his wheelchair and respirator.

What Brian thought of the prom, no one heard him say. He was characteristically taciturn about his personal feelings. But what can be surmised is that his desire to be just another kid at the prom with his best girl could not be achieved that night, or, for that matter, any night.

The Spartanburg Herald-Journal, capitalizing on the human-interest angle, assigned a reporter and photographer to cover the event. The subsequent feature-length story and photos that appeared in its pages conveyed the public impression that Brian was overcoming the effects of his impairment and returning to a normal life, which, of course, he was not.

But while quadriplegia had shaken his natural enthusiasm for a time, it failed to quash Brian's spirit entirely. In an essay for a high school English assignment, he wrote:

My original goal in life, before my accident, was to attend a good engineering school and become an aerospace engineer. To become part of a team that may send mankind into space to live was my dream. I hoped to work for either an independent firm (Lockheed, McDonnell Douglas, etc.) or NASA. . .This dream is still alive in my mind. It will be a little harder to accomplish, but I can do it.

His resolve remained strong that this physical impairment must not undermine the realization of the ambitious goals he had set for his life. Considering the achievements earlier in his disability, his confidence in the future seemed justified.

Mike Burnette recalls that on his visits to the Baco residence right after the accident, he would leave marveling at some new skill his friend had mastered. After missing an entire year of school, he returned to campus as a senior, accelerated through the curriculum, and graduated on time with his class. On commencement night, thousands of people gathered at the stadium where Brian once played soccer and stood en masse to applaud the awarding of his diploma.

Now turning his thoughts to college, Brian hoped to fulfill his dream of becoming an aerospace engineer. His first choice was Georgia Tech in Atlanta, one of the nation's premiere engineering schools. But soon the impracticality of this choice became apparent to him and his mother. Even if he earned a full academic scholarship to Georgia Tech, the family would still be confronted with the considerable expense of supporting him. To attend a university out of state would require round-the-clock nursing care as well as an assistant to accompany him to class each day. Faced with those limitations, attending college locally seemed the only reasonable alternative. Brian ultimately enrolled in the University of South Carolina at Spartanburg, the only public four-year college in the community.

USCS, which is largely a commuter college, offers a convenient and affordable post-secondary education for the average resident in Upstate South Carolina. But for a gifted student intent on designing rocket engines, the decision to enroll there represented a major concession. Intrinsic in that decision was the admission that a career in aerospace engineering had been erased from his future. Lost, as well, was the opportunity to pit his intellectual skills against other good minds in the rigorous academic setting at Georgia Tech.

What USCS did offer, though, was a degree program in computer science that was a respectable match for Brian's aptitudes and interests. Lowering the bar of his expectations to a level that seemed more achievable, he now pinned his hopes on a career in a computer-related field.

As in high school, the nurse sat with him at the back of the classroom taking notes during lectures and transcribing his oral responses to exam questions. Still, Brian continued to learn in his own inimitable way, absorbing blocks of information directly from the lectures. If anything, the inability to write seemed to enhance his gifts for retaining and analyzing data. Possessed of an uncanny ability to solve math problems in his head, Barbara often found it easier to turn to Brian for answers rather than reaching for the electronic calculator stored in her desk drawer.

On days the nurse called in sick, Barbara would sometimes take leave from work to accompany Brian to his classes. There, she observed up close the stares he had to endure from some of his fellow students who were still unaccustomed to the sight of a high-level quadriplegic. She came to appreciate even more deeply his self-consciousness about being a "spectacle," the dread with which he navigated his way around campus in the clumsy wheelchair, his desperation to be treated as a normal person, and the quiet strength with which he confronted each day knowing he was not.

She also attended Brian's logic class with him and witnessed his ease with academia. In computer labs, he was often frustrated by his inability to perform tasks manually on the keyboard that other students completed with relative ease. But in logic class, where mental acuity was the sole consideration, Brian excelled. While some of what went on in that classroom was beyond Barbara's comprehension, she saw how he was invigorated by the challenge of a logic problem and how animated he became in discussions with the instructor and other students. She was astounded by Brian's intellectual prowess, his enormous capacity to mentally storm a complex issue, break it down into its component parts, and capture the essence of it. As she watched, she was stunned by the realization that a product of her marriage to Herman was a true intellectual, at home in an academic environment in a way neither she nor any other member of their family ever would be.

Chapter 25

Meanwhile, as Elizabeth approached the end of her high school career, the frayed bond with her parents continued to unravel. The fallout wrecked her concentration and contributed to the decline of her academic performance. With tension running high around their home, Elizabeth's mother called Brian one day to accuse him of ruining Elizabeth's life. Brian listened calmly to her complaints, allowing the words to settle in without growing defensive or angry.

When Elizabeth pleaded that she was in love, her mother wondered out loud if she knew the meaning of the word, insinuating that her youth and inexperience somehow invalidated what she felt for Brian. Elizabeth could provide no satisfactory response to her mother's challenge. Who is wise or mature enough to fathom love? Elizabeth was learning to love in the only way one can—by the act of being loving. Even more impressive is the fact that in a culture fixated on beauty and virility, she dared to love a boy who would be judged by many to be an undesirable mate.

Elizabeth was backed into a bind destined to bring heartache to all concerned. In a scenario reminiscent of the Montagues and Capulets, she felt forced to choose between Brian and her family. The day after her high school graduation, she quietly gathered her possessions and fled to Brian's house.

While Barbara objected to their decision for several reasons, including the invasion of her own privacy, she says the Balarams' mistake was forbidding something as natural and inevitable as teen love, a position that made the relationship virtually irresistible. (Elizabeth claims that after she moved out her father privately conceded that they may have been overly protective of her.) Elizabeth speculates that if they had been less emphatic, she would have eventually tired of the relationship and never moved in with the Bacos at all. As it was, she set out defiantly to prove her parents wrong.

At first, life among her new allies was reasonably good. Brian found himself in the company of the two people he loved best in the world. For her part, Barbara was grateful for the extra pair of hands. Sharing responsibilities with Elizabeth freed her from some of the physical confinement that had defined her life since Brian's discharge from Shepherd Spinal Center. And Elizabeth was relieved for the sanctuary, having resolved the conflict with her parents in the way families often do: by creating physical distance.

Practically speaking, things around the house appeared to change little. But psychologically, Elizabeth's arrival signaled a subtle yet dramatic course adjustment. By taking up residence under the same roof as Brian, Elizabeth's stature grew proportionately. Now entrenched as Brian's significant other, she was assuming increasing responsibility for both his physical and emotional care. More than a girlfriend, Elizabeth had earned a promotion to partner, with all the privileges the title conferred.

As for Brian, the move forced him into the awkward position of having to choose between the two women in his life, a bind in which his mother was the likely loser. Like any young man, he gravitated instinctively to his beloved's arms. Where his mother's provision of his most intimate needs had always left him feeling self-conscious, Elizabeth's care was understood as a woman's natural expression of love for her man.

It was becoming apparent that Barbara's displacement was not likely to be negotiated without inflicting some painful grievances. Though it was natural for Brian to turn to Elizabeth, Barbara was not able to manage much perspective at the time. Her growing exclusion from her son's life played upon her lifelong struggle with abandonment and stung that wounded place in her that anticipated rejection. For years she had served as the central figure in Brian's life, a role now usurped by Elizabeth. And in this odd love triangle, Barbara became the disposable third person destined to feel unappreciated and unloved.

When tensions in the house on Runnymeade Drive escalated, a close friend questioned Barbara's passivity in the situation. How, she asked, could she allow Elizabeth to become "the controlling factor" in her own home? But the truth is, it was not Barbara's home and never had been. It was Herman's at the time of their divorce, just as surely as it now belonged to Brian and Elizabeth. Barbara found herself as the outsider, the one expected to acquiesce and accommodate.

"At that point," she says, "I was an unwanted guest. And I could either keep my mouth shut or get out."

When Elizabeth was in the house, she fed and bathed Brian. When she was absent, Barbara filled in as her substitute. With the young lovers preoccupied with each other in the front of the house, Barbara was exiled to a bedroom in the back. The emotional bond to her son remained intact, but the retreat from his physical presence grew into a painful daily reality.

The conflict was exacerbated by Elizabeth's personal issues. Baco family friends remember her as a troubled and unstable young woman. Ruby characterizes her as "a sick child," and Barbara recounts how she watched bemused one day as Elizabeth dressed the cat in doll clothes. Completely cut off from her parents and bereft of any close friendships, she now staked her entire emotional bankroll on Brian. Her neediness brought additional pressure to what, at best, was a very fragile set of circumstances.

In the process of living together, troubling signs of Elizabeth's instability began to surface. One night she became upset about something so apparently inconsequential that no one, including Elizabeth, can quite remember what it was. All efforts to appease her failed. Exploding into fury, she bolted from the house and ran down the street, screaming hysterically. The police were called, and patrol cars soon descended on the scene. Elizabeth was eventually found trembling behind a tree in the yard. She was escorted inside, where a female police officer worked for some time to calm her before she was finally taken into custody to undergo a psychiatric evaluation.

Elizabeth, accompanied by Brian, attended several sessions with a psychotherapist. But counseling, which requires a willing client, proved to be a pointless exercise. That Elizabeth got upset was not the issue, as Barbara sees it. She appreciated how the constant stress and hardship of living with someone so severely impaired could fray the nerves of even the strongest person. But it was her lack of impulse control that transformed understandable frustration into a public spectacle that alarmed the people in Brian's life and reinforced their lack of confidence in Elizabeth as his primary caregiver.

She had burst into Brian's home as an exile. She arrived with an urgent agenda to prove to her skeptical parents that she was indeed an adult. Working a full-time job and attending college part time, she tried to shoehorn these daily commitments around her growing responsibility for Brian. Barbara, who appreciated as no one else did the demands of her son's care, offered to share the load. But Elizabeth could not hear the wisdom in her charity. It was not enough to be one of several people important to Brian; she was determined to be his everything.

Elizabeth's way of coping with domestic conflict was to pout, stubbornly refusing to speak to the offending party, sometimes for days. Her sulking and nursing of minor grudges deepened animosities around the house. Ruby Craig remembers occasional "family" conferences called to address the conflict. Each individual—Barbara, Brian, Elizabeth and Ruby—was offered the opportunity to bring up concerns in hopes they might be resolved. Everyone took advantage of these occasions to speak up and clear the air except for Elizabeth. Brian, reluctant to probe too deeply into emotional issues, did not press her to participate. Whenever differences came between them, they simply withdrew from one another, leaving the resentment to fester.

Elizabeth mistook independence and self-sufficiency for maturity. Blinded by their illusions of love, neither she nor Brian could see that the real source of their strength was always in an alliance with others.

Together they succeeded in alienating the two people in the house who could have made their life together more bearable. By their conspiracy to shut Barbara and Ruby out, the young couple effectively sabotaged themselves. Under more hospitable circumstances, their love may have grown into an enduring commitment. Instead, having just fled one prison, Elizabeth soon found herself trapped in yet another.

Chapter 26

Brian was uncharacteristically passive when it came to dealing with Elizabeth. He likely appreciated the fragility of her commitment to him as well the relative weakness of the hand he was holding. If he pushed too hard, she might simply walk away. Thus, he chose to muzzle his displeasure with the relationship and conceded as best he could to her because concession was more bearable than the thought of losing her.

He felt forced to accept the relationship on her terms, hoping that if he swallowed his unhappiness and remained agreeable, she would stay. He was hostage to a relationship that was precariously unbalanced. He needed her in way she would never need him, even confessing to her once his intention to die if they were not together.

This desperation drove him to side with his girlfriend against his mother, the one person in his life whose loyalty to him was unimpeachable. Caught in the crossfire of the fierce hostility between the two women, Brian could find no cover. The couple even secretly contacted Herman to explore the option of removing Barbara from the house, a proposition to which Elizabeth says Herman gave his consent.

Ruby Craig's presence had served as a sponge to soak up some of the intensity of the situation. But Elizabeth, who perceived the beloved nurse as a threat, changed staffing services, which effectively expelled Ruby from the home. With Ruby out of the way, Barbara was left in the awkward position of living in the house with the two young lovers who coveted their privacy. She was unsure what to do. If she moved out, her son's life would be squarely in the hands of an individual she did not trust. If, on the other hand, she demanded that Elizabeth leave, she risked alienating Brian.

Paralyzed by the perplexity of the situation, she sought Sean Cullen's counsel. Over breakfast, he listened as Barbara described her dilemma. He advised against forcing Elizabeth out of the house, agreeing that it would cast Barbara as the villain. It would also provide a splint to keep the young couple's crippled relationship limping along.

Though she would be criticized for doing so, Barbara ultimately took Sean's advice. In order to salvage the relationship with her son, she left him. She packed up her belongings and grimly walked away from the house on Runnymeade Drive. Her hunch was that when she was removed as a target, Brian and Elizabeth would have no choice but to confront their unhappiness with each other.

"You can only take so much of a good thing," Barbara says, smiling wryly, "and then it starts to turn bad."

For some time, Barbara had needed a hysterectomy, but like most everything else in her personal life, it had been set aside. Now relieved of the daily obligation to Brian, she decided to proceed with the operation. Barbara's hospitalization, along with her decision to voluntarily leave the house, seemed to release the valve on Elizabeth's hostility toward her. After Barbara was discharged from the hospital, the young couple unexpectedly invited her to join them for dinner. According to Elizabeth, the evening together was tense, but ultimately proved productive. During Barbara's recovery, Elizabeth chauffeured her back and forth to the house to visit with Brian. Though Barbara appreciated the gesture, she chose to maintain her low profile, determined not to be drawn back into the conflict.

As early as the following summer, Barbara's prediction began to come true. Having conspired to run off Ruby and Barbara, their two most loyal allies, the couple's isolation was nearly complete. When Barbara removed herself as their convenient foil, Brian and Elizabeth were left to face their disillusionment with each other.

Barbara's friends, who had been conscientiously kind and encouraging of Brian, were now reluctant to visit him. With Barbara gone, visits to Runnymeade Drive felt as awkward as dropping in on newlyweds. Mike and David made regular visits during school breaks and on occasional weekends. But both friends were attending college out of state, which limited their availability. According to Ruby, Elizabeth succeeded in running off his other friends, including the Smith sisters, who had first introduced her to Brian and had once visited him nearly every afternoon. Progressively, Brian's world was shrinking, now reduced mostly to nursing replacements for Ruby and a fugitive girlfriend.

Desperate for a reliable nurse to replace Ruby, Barbara summoned her nerve and called Deborah Seay. Deborah, who had worked for the Bacos previously, was one of the nurses who resigned after being accused of stealing. She denies the charges to this day, noting that items Barbara reported missing were mostly personal effects like ashtrays and bed linens that were of no interest to her. Despite the previous unpleasantness, Brian and Deborah had always shared an affection for each other. Apart from Ruby, she was probably his favorite of all the nurses who had cared for him.

Hearing of Brian's predicament, Deborah decided to set aside her offense at Barbara's accusations and return to the Bacos' employment. But as a divorcee bearing her own slew of personal issues, she added further intrigue to the churning domestic crisis. She fanned Elizabeth's natural curiosity about dating with tales of her own exploits as a single woman.

"How many guys have you dated?" Deborah asked Elizabeth one day, deciding to press the subject.

"Not many," Elizabeth replied shyly. "Brian's my first serious relationship."

"You know there are a lot of fish in the sea, a lot of fish in the sea."

"Yeah, but I love Brian."

"Darlin', I know that feeling. But how can you know for sure it's the real thing if you haven't dated some other guys?"

Elizabeth had already begun to wrestle with her predicament, and Deborah's questions planted more seeds of doubt. She was now older and less naïve about the impracticalities of being a lifelong partner to Brian. So when Deborah appeared, regaling her with stories of the single life, Elizabeth listened. It was not so much that Deborah's opinions persuaded Elizabeth, as they confirmed conclusions she had reached herself. She was hungry for new experiences that did not include the daily grind of being yoked to a severely impaired man. Furthermore, she was feeling the strain of the self-imposed exile from her parents. As she herself admitted, Brian might or might not be her boyfriend, but her parents were always her parents.

Elizabeth insists love was never the issue on Runnymeade Drive. She says that she never stopped loving Brian and that her departure was mostly about timing and being an inexperienced twenty-year-old. After near suffocation at home and confinement on Runnymeade Drive, she ached to be free. There was a voyage of self-discovery before her on which Brian could not accompany her. She wanted to go. She needed to go. And yet she was trapped in a predicament of her own making: How could she gracefully abandon a desperately injured boyfriend to whom she had pledged her love? His confession that he would die without her added greatly to the burden of guilt she bore. She was torn between her loyalty to him and an equally compelling commitment to herself.

Elizabeth confided in a young man she worked with at a local department store. The secrets they exchanged created a sense of intimacy that evolved into a predictable infatuation. The two co-workers leaned on each other, forming an emotional attachment that reinforced her unhappiness with Brian.

Ruby and Deborah both recall overhearing her late-night phone conversations after Brian had been put to bed, with Elizabeth whispering into the receiver in the hushed tones of a paramour. Elizabeth insists she was consoling a female co-worker being abused by her husband. Ruby, however, tells of an irate woman appearing at the house one evening to accuse Elizabeth of having an affair with her husband. Whether Brian was conscious of this possible betrayal is unclear, but he was well aware of the growing gulf between them reflected in long, awkward silences. In time, it felt less awkward to be apart, and Elizabeth fell into the habit of leaving early for work and returning home late.

Brian was faced with a bind of his own. He engaged in some heated exchanges with Elizabeth when she was late coming home, interpreting her chronic tardiness as a flagging interest in him. He desperately wanted her to stay, yet he could not compose a single compelling reason why she should. The dilemma, tiresomely familiar to him, would be reenacted with every single person who was important to him. Those upon whom he depended were required to make sacrifices on his behalf that made them resentful and him beholden, which left him perpetually torn between a desire to hold on and a sense of duty that suggested he let them go. He realized if Elizabeth stayed, she was condemning herself to a life of exceeding hardship and personal sacrifice. He longed to cling to her, but he knew the day was approaching when he would have to set her free.

A conflicted Elizabeth, unable to say goodbye, became sloppy and neglectful instead. Her behavior toward the end was especially egregious. When Brian asked her one day to change the channel on the television, she scoffed, "Change it yourself!" and stomped off.

She withheld his meals and forgot to buy groceries. Deborah had to bring food from home for him to eat. She also neglected to change his clothes or regularly clean his trach. Arriving home late many nights, she disregarded the appointed time for his daily care. The modest government check Brian received each month was now directly deposited into Elizabeth's checking account. Funds intended for his personal care were instead used for her personal and household purchases. According to Ruby, Elizabeth, by her actions, had already abandoned Brian.

Novelist Kathryn Harrison writes that, "Some love makes the world less safe," a sentiment to which Brian could attest. He felt forlorn. Nothing in his previous experience of this woman with whom he had once shared such tenderness had prepared him for the arrival of her evil twin. He could not bear to believe that Elizabeth would act with such reckless disregard for his feelings and safety. Yet he could not bear to break it off with her. Barbara doubts he ever would have. Instead, he sat passively by, awaiting an outcome he felt powerless to reverse.

While Deborah encouraged Elizabeth to explore her options, she also reported her trespasses to Barbara. As the story of neglect began to unfold, Barbara's maternal instincts eventually overrode her respect for her son's privacy. She went to Brian and confronted him directly about the allegations reported to her, which he confirmed. At that point, Barbara had had enough. What they as a couple lacked the resolve to do themselves, she would intervene to do on her son's behalf.

Over Elizabeth's protests, Barbara had her expelled from the house. When Deborah reported to Barbara that Elizabeth was trying to remove possessions, including a family bookcase, Barbara put her foot down.

"You tell her not to take that bookcase out of the house," she instructed Deborah. "She's taken all she's going to take."

Reasserting her rightful role as matriarch, she returned to the Runnymeade residence with suitcase in hand and a renewed sense of purpose as her son's advocate. Only this time, the stay would be temporary. No longer willing to abide dependence on Herman, who except for paying the mortgage had been largely absent from the ordeal, she was prepared to transfer Brian to her home on White Oak Street.

But there was a problem. Her home was not equipped to accommodate Brian's wheelchair, and Barbara didn't have the resources to remodel it.

One day during a break at work she was crying softly on the employee deck, when a co-worker named Gordon approached to console her. Barbara explained her predicament to him and he offered to help. For $300 cash and a diamond ring that belonged to Barbara's mother, Gordon, who did handyman projects on the side, agreed to build a ramp and a deck on the back of the house and install a backdoor wide enough for the wheelchair and additional electric outlets to support Brian's equipment.

Elizabeth was by then a nursing student at the local university. With only part-time employment and nowhere to live, she visited her parents to explore the possibility of returning home to live. The Balarams agreed she could return to the house under the condition that she must observe their rules. But Elizabeth, who was now an adult, was even less willing to bend to their authority than before and refused. Instead, she temporarily moved in with a friend. Meanwhile, the relationship with her boyfriend intensified and eventually culminated in their decision to marry.

For a time, Elizabeth tried to renew ties with Brian, but Barbara, fearing a possible reconciliation, instructed the nurses to report any contact between the two of them. One afternoon, Elizabeth dropped by ostensibly to share with Brian her enthusiasm about an anatomy class in which she was enrolled. Her motives for the visit were unclear even in her own mind. However, their conversation was abruptly cut off by the appearance of the nurse on duty who, under orders from Barbara, asked her to leave. Elizabeth turned to Brian, hoping for some sign of protest against this indignity, but there was none. As the door closed behind her that day, it was with a sense of finality. It was to be the last time Elizabeth would ever see Brian.

Chapter 27

Brian was left to make peace with a grief that seemed inconsolable. To most people, including his mother, he would never utter Elizabeth's name again, a fact that Barbara attributes to old-fashioned practicality.

"When it's over, it's over," she observes.

But the truth is that it wasn't over. Brian would speak of Elizabeth again but mostly in private conversations with Deborah Seay. When Barbara was away, he would sometimes grow sullen and even on occasion unburden himself in tears. Deborah appreciated his grief and listened attentively, his sorrow intermingling and resonating with her own.

They clung to one another as confidantes, and out of their mutual sharing, a close friendship evolved. With Deborah, Brian felt free to express the sense of loss he dared not reveal to his mother. With her, he carefully replayed the events as they had unfolded, reminiscing about the early euphoric days of their romance, followed by his growing frustration with how little he had to offer Elizabeth physically, and finally the crushing disappointment of her departure. The question that would torment his curious mind for months to come was: Why? Why did things turn out so badly? Why weren't two people who claimed to love one another able to reconcile their differences? He would never arrive at any satisfactory answer to those questions, of course, but it was apparently important to ask and, what's more, that there be someone present to hear his questions.

If the first major transition of Brian Baco's life was defined by the injury itself, then the second began with Elizabeth's departure. Even after the accident and prior to his girlfriend's arrival, Brian had been distinguished by his exuberance for and mastery over life. Whatever he set his mind to do, he did.

Then came Elizabeth. She was the litmus test of his post-injury potential. If he could enchant a beautiful girl without command of his body, then perhaps he really could have anything he wanted. However, it wasn't the breakup with Elizabeth that challenged that assumption so much as the daily ordeal of trying to live with her. Elizabeth broke his heart, exposing his vulnerabilities in a way that he had not experienced since his brush with the medical profession. He was humiliated each day by the frequent reminders of all that life with him denied her and the corresponding realization there wasn't one damn thing he could do about it. For once in Brian's life, mind over matter failed him. No matter how determined he was, he could not will the relationship to turn out happily.

When Barbara returned to him, she observed a change in his disposition. He seemed more sober and less resilient than before. Elizabeth's rejection had sapped his reserve of optimism. Part of him appeared to die with their goodbye, never to be revived again. The recycled version of this young man was more humble than before as well as less confident in his ability to cope with life's vicissitudes. Dispatched for good were any former illusions of overcoming the injury. He was now mindful, as perhaps he never had been before, that there were plans for his life that might be out of his reach—a sobering reality for a person of only 21 years of age to have to swallow.

The dissolution of the relationship set in motion a series of disappointments that would define the last stage of Brian's life. First, he was forced to move into his mother's compact house. Even though his father's name appeared on the mortgage of the Runnymeade Drive property, in his absence, Brian could fancy himself as lord of the manse. Living there with his girlfriend boosted his image of himself as a normal, healthy male. Conversely, moving to his mother's house signified the loss of that status. While grateful to be rescued from

Elizabeth's neglect, he regretted the return to his dependence on Barbara. Friends who had survived Elizabeth's possessive ways now had another reason to avoid him. Only individuals with enduring bonds, like David and Mike, bothered to seek him out on White Oak Street.

The move also cost him the relationship with Ruby Craig. Barbara tried to persuade Brian to have Ruby come back to work for the family, but he refused. While he never explained why, it isn't too difficult to assume that he was ashamed of himself for allowing Elizabeth to dismiss her. Ruby continued to call periodically to check on Brian, but there would never again be the daily contact between them that had helped sustain him.

In addition, Brian was forced to confront how Elizabeth had damaged his relationship with Barbara. He had chosen Elizabeth over his mother, and the two had all but banished her from the house. Deborah recalls there being a chilly distance between mother and son, a distance that would take time to heal.

There were other indications of the deterioration of Brian's condition. While he continued his studies at USCS, his college experience was made more difficult by Sharon, his first-shift nurse at the time. Brian felt considerable contempt for her partly because she had succeeded Ruby Craig, whose prominence in his life almost no one could be expected to match. But Sharon contributed to his hard feelings by her tendency to sleep on the job as well as a habit of bringing her daughter and later her granddaughter to work with her. Her behavior represented both a breach of professional conduct and an invasion of his privacy.

Part of Sharon's responsibility was to escort Brian to class each day. But after he enrolled in a biology course, she declared she would take no part in any lab assignments involving animal dissection. Whether it was truly her duty to assist with dissections is debatable, but the contrast between Sharon's attitude and the memory of Ruby dragging him and his wheelchair down to the beach was striking.

While a federal Pell Grant paid the cost of Brian's tuition, it did not cover the cost of books, parking, and other school-related expenses. To make matters worse, in completing the grant application, Barbara improperly included his monthly disability check as income, effectively reducing the amount of grant money for which he qualified. Like trying to finance a Cadillac on a Chevy income, the cost of college began to impose itself on the family's modest budget. After two years of absorbing various incidental fees, the Baco treasury was depleted.

Lacking funds to purchase books for his course work, Brian withdrew from school before the start of the first semester of his junior year. In retrospect, Barbara says she regrets not working harder to identify other funding sources to supplement the Pell Grant. But with her central focus on keeping her son alive, his college education, like so many other things, got shortchanged.

The sabbatical from school left Brian time to assess the state of his predicament, and, ultimately, he concluded that like the inevitable breakup with Elizabeth, he was probably unemployable. The two-year stint at USCS had illustrated the limitations of his reach. To work, he would first have to locate an employer willing to absorb the expense of purchasing special equipment as well as one who would accommodate the special needs of an employee with high-level quadriplegia. His ongoing medical problems meant he was likely to exceed the number of sick days permitted, and it was impossible to predict what his condition might do to the premiums of a company's health care insurance policy.

But the clincher may have been the realization that his disability was a condition he would never outgrow. Wherever Brian's adventures in life took him, the flight could never be solo. The respirator had seen to that. Someone, whether it was Barbara or a nurse, would have to be constantly at his side. And who was going to bear the cost of having a caregiver accompany him to a job, whether that job was in an office or out of his home? Regardless of how sophisticated the technology or how skilled he was at manipulating it, there would always be tasks as elementary as turning the pages of a report or opening a door that he could not do for himself. No matter how much he strived or how far he stretched, life as an independent adult would always remain beyond his reach.

Casting about for something solid to sustain him, Brian found instead an awful, aching void. Sharon's vacant gaze mirrored that of an indifferent world closing in on him. Whether he was literally unemployable or not is debatable; disability rights activists would likely take exception with this conclusion. The New England Journal of Medicine reports that "overall, from 34 to 58 percent of persons with spinal cord injuries become involved in competitive employment." But the statistic fails to cite how many of these individuals had sustained injuries as severe as Brian's.

A counselor with the office of Vocational Rehabilitation in South Carolina says that in the early 1990s, Brian would not have passed the department's screening process to determine qualified job applicants. Although Voc Rehab now accepts cases involving more severe emotional and physical disabilities, its program remains skewed toward those with the greatest potential for employment. Comparing Brian's case to others, the counselor characterized Brian's vocational prospects as "very limited."

There are federal matching grants to subsidize an employer's expense in hiring a disabled person and technology programs by which engineers design adaptive tools to equip disabled persons to perform necessary tasks on the job. But living in a small town without skilled and determined advocates to champion his cause left Brian at a distinct disadvantage in the marketplace.

Brian's ambition began to clash with his limitations, assailing his instinct for survival. For an individual with more modest expectations, a comfortable roof over one's head and a television for entertainment might be enough. There is surely a correlation between what one asks of life and one's level of satisfaction with it—and Brian Baco demanded a lot. His appetite and curiosity were too robust to survive indefinitely on a steady diet of reruns and computer games.

With his losses mounting, Brian faced a serious question: What remains to give me reason to get out of bed and meet the day? With both Elizabeth and Ruby now gone from his life and the promise of meaningful employment remote, the search for an answer turned up nothing. Those who have been there can attest that despair is an insidious thing. It drowns hope and determination in its malignant sea of purposelessness.

Chapter 28

Lack of funds was the stated reason for Brian's withdrawal from USCS. But money alone was, at best, only a mild deterrent. If his heart had been set on earning a college degree, Barbara surely would have scraped up the funds to pay for it. Instead, the decision to withdraw may have been symptomatic of something darker—a sign that Brian Baco was beginning to surrender to insurmountable circumstances.

Brian did not so much drop out of school as he allowed the temporary leave to lapse into a permanent one, stripping him of critical intellectual stimulation and association with his peers. The passivity with which he allowed this to happen seemed uncharacteristic for him. It was likely an expression of despair. And like all acts of desperation, it was a decision that lacked any serious consideration of its long-term implications.

Still, money was to remain an issue for the family. Linda Ashley expresses amazement that Barbara could make so little go so far. Barbara's modest wages from her clerical job and Brian's monthly $270 Supplemental Security Income (SSI) check were the only two reliable sources of income. Between the divorce and Brian's disability, the family's standard of living had slipped precipitously from middle-class comfort to a more austere urban grittiness. Gone were the days of pool memberships, summer vacations, and allowances for new clothes.

Resourcefulness became the rule. The White Oak Road house

had no air conditioning. Brian, whose internal thermostat was damaged by his injury, was trapped in the heat and suffering terribly. Barbara lacked the funds to do anything about it, but persuaded her mother to give them an old window unit. After it broke, she replaced it with another unit borrowed from a friend. Eventually, Barbara obtained a low-interest loan from the city for low-income families that she used to install central air, along with vinyl siding and a new roof.

The care of a quadriplegic can run into the millions of dollars over the course of a lifetime, threatening many families with bankruptcy. Though no one's contentment with life can be measured strictly in financial terms, a member of the ethics committee at Shepherd Center acknowledged that "money does make a difference" when it comes to the degree of hardship disabled people must endure. Affluence can purchase reliable, competent, round-the-clock nursing care, state-of-the-art technology, and comprehensive insurance coverage, all of which make living conditions more bearable for the disabled person and his family. There have been astounding advances in technology to support a greater degree of independence for individuals with spinal cord injuries, everything from voice-activated computers to mechanisms that turn the pages of books, but it is all academic without the means to acquire and maintain them.

The community's fund-raising effort, which had proven crucial in defraying the family's initial expenses, was now dried up. Brian's support system was hemorrhaging badly. The steady stream of visitors who had greeted him upon his return from Atlanta was now reduced to a trickle.

The causes of the erosion of support were several. For one thing, it reflected the chaotic state of affairs on White Oak Road. "The whole house was crazy," one friend recalls. During the Elizabeth era there had been enough petty conflict and intrigue to make the residents of Peyton Place blush. Brian and Elizabeth tended to keep their unhappiness to themselves, but Barbara regularly vented her frustration about her son's girlfriend, what one individual characterized as "going off the deep end." In time, friends who had grown weary of the conflict first avoided the subject, then later steered clear of the house.

But the lack of visitors was also the natural byproduct of former high school friends preoccupied with building personal and professional lives of their own. Simply put, Brian was a victim of friends who were growing up. Some of his old inner circle was physically removed from Spartanburg, either attending school or working jobs out of town. Despite the fact that it reflected a normal developmental stage in the process of growing up, it did not keep Brian from experiencing their absence as a personal desertion. He was hurt that they no longer stopped by to talk or play computer games, but more than that, he mourned the sense of being left behind.

In a rambling note to Brian, a high school buddy named Diane opens with a description of her life as "pretty blah," but proceeds to describe details that seem anything but. She writes of being awarded a graduate assistantship worth $7,500, a stormy relationship with a boyfriend named Robbie, a hectic schedule that has kept her from visiting home for more than half a day since she left for school, and a promise to call the next time she was in town. The content of the letter includes one lone, breezy reference to Brian and his condition: "How are you doing? I hope everything is going well."

Intended to convey support, the letter likely had exactly the opposite effect. It struck where Brian was most vulnerable: the loss of his girlfriend and evaporation of career opportunities. It also succeeded in reinforcing what he already knew. While his young adult friends were out reveling at parties, making love, going to football games and the beach, he could never join them.

"Years go by, and what do I have?" he once lamented. "I have a TV, a jam box, and a nurse."

Diane was representative of many who were torn between the guilt-induced obligation to go see Brian and the equally compelling inclination to stay away. To be sure, the Baco home was not a place for the fainthearted. There was survivor's guilt that left many visitors feeling they should apologize to Brian for their freedom of movement. There was also the ever-present temptation of succumbing to sweet-sounding platitudes in a situation where people faltered to find anything encouraging to say. "I know how you feel," rang especially hollow coming from anyone who could walk in through the front door under his or her own power. Shaking hands, a custom designed to break down awkward barriers when two people first meet, was, of course, not an option with Brian. And to have touched his face, the one part of his body where he still had feeling, was reserved only for those who shared the most intimate relations with him.

To be in Brian's presence then, was to be naked. It was to know the utter helplessness of facing life's cruelties without the protection of familiar conventions. There was nothing that anyone could do to rescue, fix, remedy, or repair the havoc quadriplegia had wreaked.

Therefore, an encounter with Brian was an opportunity for personal growth of the highest order. It meant facing one's own personal limitations without saying or doing something inanely stupid or insensitive. And the less frequent one's visits to the Baco household, the more stressful the visits tended to be. Barbara Tassin, a close friend of the family, admits to the internal battle she fought to make herself spend time with Brian when it would have been easier to simply stay away.

But the awkwardness many people experienced was not Brian's doing. In fact, he worked hard as a host to create a hospitable environment to ensure his guests would come back. Yet, at the same time, his receptors were keenly sensitive to pity and ingratiation—dual strategies often employed by the uninitiated. He bristled, for instance, when visitors cooed how brave he was.

Being in his company involved a delicate balancing act between being sensitive and inclusive. The two individuals outside the family who were most successful at striking that balance were his friends David and Mike. They succeeded by visiting frequently enough to work through their personal discomfort with his impairment, and they possessed the wisdom to relate to Brian no differently after the injury than they had before it.

But they also enjoyed an advantage some of us did not share: a well-established relationship with him prior to the accident. David and Brian could sling insults at one another with a natural ease, what they called "busting one another's chops." And Mike refused to allow the disability to keep him from inviting Brian to serve as an honorary groomsman in his wedding, an invitation his friend enthusiastically accepted.

For others, though, the challenge of being with Brian was more difficult. A family friend, Greg Lynch, admitted he was sometimes conscious of keeping conversations with Brian superficial because he wasn't sure he wanted the "responsibility of his friendship." The discomfort with Brian's condition even infiltrated the medical profession. A physician who was removing Brian's ingrown toenails one day inexplicably began the procedure by injecting his paralyzed foot with a painkiller.

Isolation is a universal sadness that patients with long-term illnesses and injuries must endure. Their physical decline smells too much of death. Better to keep moving, keep the conversation light and the contact brief.

Paul Choberka was among those who adopted this approach. Brian and Paul had formed a close friendship years earlier over their mutual passion for soccer. Funny and fun-loving, Paul was the mirror image of his teammate. "Paul and Brian were so close," says Barbara. "When they were out on the soccer field, I had a hard time telling them apart."

But Barbara also acknowledges Paul's playful exterior, like Brian's, is a veneer hiding a deeply vulnerable core. Paul, who was with Brian the night he was injured, was "devastated" by what happened, perhaps more so than anyone outside the immediate family. After the accident, he was unable to cope with what had happened to his close friend and stopped coming to the house to visit. His desertion hurt Brian deeply and caused a bitter rift between them that went unresolved. "By staying away," says Barbara, "he never learned to deal with it."

According to Barbara Tassin, Paul eventually drifted to the coast, where he adopted the nickname of "Pablo" and led a beachcomber lifestyle. For some time, she received infrequent phone calls from him in the middle of the night. Under the influence of alcohol, he confessed to Barbara his remorse for what had happened to his friend.

To make matters worse, Herman Baco remained conspicuously

absent throughout all of this disruption. Where Barbara tended to overreact, Herman was the classic minimizer. Always a salesman, he preferred to gloss over unpleasant details and focus instead on what he perceived as the positive. He supposedly admitted to a family friend that he had distanced himself from the family because the sight of seeing his son in that condition was too painful for him.

But despite the distancing, Brian maintained a son's devotion. For most of the years of his disability, he sought to involve Herman in his life. He initiated contact by phone and made personal visits to Florida that were seldom reciprocated. Where Herman was concerned, Brian seemed to have an unusually high threshold for disappointment.

From his home in Florida and later in Louisiana, Herman excused his absence as a matter of logistics. But he failed in other, more tangible ways to convey love and support. There was, for example, neglect of maintenance to the Runnymeade Drive property he owned. The dishwasher was broken at the time Barbara separated from Herman, and it was still broken after she returned there to live with Brian. Friends contributed the money to replace the hot water heater, for which Herman, to Barbara's embarrassment, never got around to reimbursing them. He promised to pay the insurance premiums on a Cobra policy for his son, but later reneged. And he wasn't available when Brian needed money for college.

A friend privately questions whether Barbara would have been receptive had Herman taken more of an interest in their son. But that interest was seldom shown.

"You could see the frustration in Barbara's eyes," Jan Brown recalls. "It was 24/7 for her. Herman just kind of skated through it."

Herman, however, maintains he was always present for Brian, just a phone call away. But the evidence simply does not bear that out. Brian bore up under his father's neglect without complaint. He overlooked the slights on those weekends when Herman promised to visit, only to cancel at the last minute because something had come up at work. But in time, Brian surrendered to what he could not change. And the delicate bond between father and son slipped into a quiet state of inertia.

Chapter 29

B eginning with the incident at Shepherd concerning purchase of a sip and puff wheelchair, Barbara engaged in episodic battles with the insurance company over reimbursements.

Given the staggering cost of his care, Brian Baco was a liability that no company voluntarily wanted to assume. When Herman was dismissed by his employer in Pensacola, the insurer seized upon its escape clause. Herman, as well as his beneficiaries, had their group health insurance cancelled.

Brian qualified for protection under a Cobra policy that would extend his benefits for an additional eighteen months, though the family was obliged to pay the premiums. But beyond that, his prospects for finding medical insurance appeared grim. He failed to qualify for coverage under Herman's new insurance plan because his condition was pre-existing, and the purchase of a private policy would have been prohibitively expensive.

Without insurance coverage, Brian could qualify for Medicaid. But its regulations at the time did not permit the family's employment of private duty nurses, leaving Barbara to contemplate only two available options: placing Brian permanently in a hospital or a residential care facility. But Shepherd Spinal Center could supply the names of only two nursing homes on the entire East Coast that at the time were accepting respirator-dependent patients. With the clock ticking down toward the expiration of the Cobra policy, Brian was facing institutionalization. Barbara vowed to sell the house and relocate with him, but it would hardly be the same.

Complicating matters was the breakdown of Brian's overall health. Immediately following the accident, medical professionals had worked to stabilize Brian's condition. It was a tenuous stability that would never again be easy to maintain. For all the enormous courage and determination he displayed, Brian was now helpless to reverse the physical wreckage of a body no longer capable of coping with multiple systemic failures. That realization led his pulmonary specialist, Charles Fogarty, to privately express doubt that his young patient would survive the next year.

For one thing, Brian was susceptible to kidney infections. And like all non-ambulatory patients, he was subject to developing hideous bedsores that would become infected and were nearly impossible to heal. His lungs functioned well for the most part, but there was always the threat of developing pneumonia, a condition that would have seriously threatened his life.

For an entire year he was bed-bound with severe spasms that originated in his back and extended down the length of both legs. The doctor explained these involuntary movements to Barbara as incomplete messages originating in his brain to which his body responded with confusion. Either lying in bed or seated in his wheelchair, the spasms would appear without warning, causing his legs to convulse erratically. The jerking movement was so violent that Barbara or the nurse had to apply pressure to his feet to keep him from hurting himself. Only after a surgical procedure to sever the nerves to the legs did the condition improve.

There was also damage to his internal thermostat. According to Dr. William Bockenek, spinal cord patients are susceptible to poikilothermia, a state more commonly known as cold-bloodedness. The neurological damage caused by a spinal cord injury disrupts the brain's signals to the outlying nerves so that just as the brain can no longer command the muscles to move, it also loses control over regulation of the body's temperature, a task it usually manages by sending signals to the blood vessels to dilate or contract in response to climatic changes. With the internal thermostat disarmed, his body temperature now approximated the temperature around him. When the air circulating around him was warm, his body temperature rose, and, likewise, when it was cold, he was, too. The inability to regulate body temperature by perspiring or shivering left him susceptible to both hypothermia and heat stroke. His caregivers had to monitor changes and either add layers of clothing or remove them to compensate for what his body could no longer do for itself.

Besides the danger to his health, Brian was hyper-sensitive to even moderately cool weather. He compensated by keeping a space heater positioned to blow directly into his face.

On the other hand, he loved the summertime, basking in the backyard soaking up the sun's warmth like a lizard perched on a rock. The excessive sunbathing turned the skin on his face and hands a deep shade of copper. But the exposure to the ultra-violet light was so intense that it managed to penetrate his clothing, tanning most of his unexposed flesh as well.

Besides the aversion to cold, Brian was tormented by chronic phantom pain in his limbs. It was most excruciating in the big toe of his right foot, a relentless throbbing sensation that he compared to being "smashed with a hammer." Ironically, he experienced the bizarre pairing of lost sensation and acute pain. The injured spine was guilty of playing the cruelest trick of all upon him. Generous in its receptivity to suffering, it was altogether indifferent to the sensation of pleasure.

Even more health problems were to follow. Deborah observed that Brian was sweating profusely and developing a large number of bedsores. Afraid his kidneys were shutting down, she insisted he be taken to the hospital for examination. He was angry with her and agreed only grudgingly to go.

The resulting lab report pinpointed the cause. Brian's blood sugar level had risen to a reading of 700 (100 is considered normal), putting him at risk of slipping into a coma. Even exhibiting all the classic symptoms, excessive sweating, extreme thirst, and chronic weakness, neither he nor his mother was prepared for the diagnosis of diabetes mellitus. In spite of having a family history of the disease, a doctor speculated that its onset may have been accelerated by the spinal cord injury.

When he was diagnosed and learned that amputation of limbs was a possible consequence, Brian turned to Deborah and whispered, "Just let me die. I'm not going to live and let them cut off my legs and arms."

Injections of insulin twice a day regulated Brian's blood sugar level. He refused to watch when the shots were being administered, despite the fact he could not feel the prick of the needle penetrating his skin. Ever since the accident, this formerly macho male had developed an aversion to all forms of human suffering. Barbara recalls how he would divert his eyes whenever images of violence or misery appeared on television.

But the injections were a mild inconvenience compared to diabetes' impact on his eating habits. Brian was placed on a strict diet that forbid sweets and fried foods. The treatment plan worked well, returning his blood sugar level to the normal range, but it was bought at a price. The ability to taste food and enjoy its texture in his mouth was one of the few pleasures quadriplegia had not managed to take from him. With everything else in his life collapsing around him, food remained the one abiding source of emotional comfort. He coped with the tedious progression of days by anticipating meals and snacks. Barbara, who describes food as "our refuge" from depression, had joined her son in his repast and gained fifty excess pounds herself.

Food was serious business in the Baco household, which explains Brian's irritability with meals that were not served on time or to his satisfaction. Unfortunately, the Southern cuisine that had sustained him for so long, with its emphasis on fat, salt, and sugar, was the very thing that complicated his diabetes. The cheeseburgers, milkshakes, biscuits, and gravy that he loved contributed to his growing girth and were the very foods he now had to forego to save his life. Accustomed by now to disappointment, Brian accepted this loss as he had all the others with a quiet resignation. But it also reinforced a conclusion gathering force inside him that he was being asked to inhabit a body that was no longer inhabitable.

Chapter 30

For much of his confinement, the computer had faithfully served Brian as a valuable tool. It opened the door to a vast outside world of people and ideas. The emulator board provided him a refreshing sense of independence, allowing him to operate the computer without the aid of another person.

But the apparatus eventually fell into disrepair, and lacking the funds to have it fixed, the computer's value to him was diminished. The commands he previously gave the machine using a penlight attached to his head, now required a set of hands, and the hands to whom he naturally turned belonged to Barbara. While she worked, Brian sat idly for hours pondering all that he wanted to do upon her return. For her, this nightly obligation felt mostly like a ball and chain. After long days toiling over a computer terminal at work, she returned home to find Brian waiting, eager for her to perform the same service for him.

There is, of course, no description that does justice to the multitude of indignities Brian suffered as a disabled person. To be paralyzed in a restless, mobile society that reveres freedom of movement was bad enough. But then to be strapped into a wheelchair and tethered to a noisy respirator only intensified his feelings of being a spectacle. At Shepherd he was shuttled to shopping malls to desensitize him to the public scrutiny he was sure to encounter, but it did not insulate him from the reaction of a woman in a restaurant who was so revolted by the sight of him she demanded to change tables, nor from a doctor who burst into his hospital room with guests present, threw back the bed sheets, and began to examine his nude body without so much as an "excuse me."

Dehumanization is a sad tale virtually every disabled person can tell. Some, like Dave Webb, are armed with enough ego strength to deflect the cruelty and carry on. But Brian was always sensitive to the painful whispers and stares. He never managed to lay down the former image of himself and to embrace his disability. Perhaps others were uncomfortable in his presence, in part, because he never outgrew seeing himself as damaged goods, or a "freak," as he sometimes described himself. He loved going to movies, in part because the darkness of the theater shielded him from people staring.

Each Christmas season, Brian insisted on shopping for gifts for his friends. But his Christmas spirit invariably conflicted with his self-consciousness. To make the experience more bearable, Barbara would drive him thirty miles to the mall in Greenville where he was less likely to encounter someone he knew.

"It was always a struggle," she recalls. "He never liked people looking at him."

His self-consciousness was most apparent in the presence of children. Their natural curiosity and lack of inhibition made him a magnet for their attention. In one respect, children were representative of the public in general. To encounter someone with Brian's level of incapacity was rare. No matter how discreet people tried to be, their curiosity often got the better of them. On occasion, he tried to counter the attention he attracted with reason. One day Emily Horton introduced her young grandson, Kyle, to Brian. The child responded to the sight of the strange man by running from him in fear. Upset by the reaction, Brian asked Emily to retrieve the boy so that he could talk with him. His patience eventually helped the timid child relax.

Yet not all the indignity Brian suffered was at the hands of other people. It was also the result of normal bodily functions he could no longer control. Sometimes in public he suffered the embarrassment of diarrhea. On other occasions his bladder failed him. As Brian was being offloaded from the van the night of Mike Burnette's wedding rehearsal, the condom catheter attached to his penis broke free, soaking his clothes and wheelchair in his own urine. Barbara threw a towel across his lap, and they proceeded on to the rehearsal dinner as though nothing had happened.

At times, urine ran down the frame of the wheelchair and collected on the battery and the tray that housed the respirator. Barbara and the nurses cleaned up as best they could, but ultimately no amount of scrubbing and sanitizing could rid the chair of the pungent odor permeating it. The respirator tray, which was rusted, was replaceable, but with a price tag of $1,000, the cost made it prohibitively expensive.

Though these were accidents plain and simple, they reinforced Brian's general frustration and humiliation with his condition. By the time I arrived on the scene in the summer of 1993, Brian's carefree, optimistic self no longer existed. In its place, I found a sober young man who had had enough of life and was plotting to put an end to it.

One afternoon Barbara invited me into the home to moderate a discussion between the two of them regarding his wish to die. I immediately sensed that my relationship with the family was about to take an unanticipated turn from that of a volunteer on the periphery of their lives to a supporting player in the drama about to unfold. I cannot say whether the Bacos realized the nature of our relationship had changed, but I was about to be bound to their lives in a way that far exceeded the help I had originally agreed to give.

Because Brian identified himself as an atheist and Barbara was alienated from her Catholic church, I slipped into the theological void in the familiar role of minister. I don't know that Brian would have ever intentionally sought the services of the clergy, but as Ralph Waldo Emerson observed long ago, a religious impulse burns within each of us that instinctively assigns meaning to our existence. This religious instinct is no respecter of what we believe or don't believe about God. People of faith must wrestle with their doubts, just as people who pride themselves on the power of their reason are left to ponder mysteries the mind cannot comprehend.

Brian's declaration of atheism did not make him immune to

Emerson's religious impulse. Barbara, who had grown up in a Southern Baptist church and later converted to Catholicism, was weaned on the efficacy of intercessory prayer. She brought that practice into her marriage with Herman and instilled it in her children. So it wasn't surprising that from the time Brian was very young, he habitually came to his mother when he was troubled or hurt to ask her to pray for him. Their ritual continued even after his accident. When he was in serious physical pain, he still found it comforting to invite Barbara to place her hand on his face and offer up a prayer on his behalf.

If there was ever a person who needed spiritual support, it was Brian Baco. Having endured quadriplegia for seven years and finding the existence it left him with short on meaning, he was prepared to let it go. While the decision seemed reasonable in his own mind, it was not bound to attract much sympathy in a solidly conservative community, where matters of life and death are assumed to be the domain of God.

If he was serious about following through on his plan to die, he needed his mother as an ally. In the conversation that day, Brian made his case for the advantages of terminating life support.

"I'm tired of this," he explained. "There's no point to living this way."

"How can you say that, Brian?" Barbara pleaded.

"I can say it because it's true. And you know it."

"No it's not. I love you. I don't want you to leave."

"There's no point to this," he reiterated, the level of frustration growing in his voice.

What I experienced that day were two people in an impossible bind who cared deeply for one another. He tried desperately to reason with her, explaining that dying was the only rational response to a life so short on quality. He proposed that his death promised a win/win outcome, simultaneously liberating both of them from the tyranny of quadriplegia. By letting go, he would get permanent relief from the endless suffering and she would gain her life back.

While no one appreciated the depth of her son's suffering any better than Barbara, the news of his plan still stunned her. He had spent many months, perhaps even years, contemplating this decision, but it was a revelation to her. No one loved Brian any better than did Barbara, and no one would have to struggle more to let him go.

As tense as their conversation was that day, I felt a particular privilege in being invited to witness it. I could see that each felt thwarted by the other. Brian coveted his mother's blessings. Barbara needed some acknowledgement that he was asking a lot of her. On that particular day, they would not get all the way to understanding. But out of their differences, a tenuous alliance would begin to form, a solidarity that would strengthen, coalesce, and ultimately reach its fulfillment.

Chapter 31

As it turned out, Barbara would be the least of Brian's problems. Some weeks later, I attended a consultation between the Bacos and Dr. Charles Fogarty. Fogarty appreciated the family's dilemma, was strongly supportive of Brian's right to terminate his life, and had even agreed to participate in removing him from life support. He informed the family that due to the unusual circumstances of the case he had consulted with the county coroner, Jim Burnett. The two men recall very different versions of their conversation, however. In his report later to the hospital's ethics committee, Fogarty insinuated the coroner had rejected the patient's request: "When I discussed the plan of withdrawing the ventilator at home with the coroner's office, I was informed that under current South Carolina law, this would be considered assisted suicide or possibly homicide."

Fogarty went on to contest the coroner's interpretation of the law by citing medical ethics literature confirming the right of a mentally competent patient to refuse medical treatment even at the risk of death.

The coroner, a congenial man who loves stock car racing, recalls no such conflict with the doctor. He claims to have explained to Fogarty that Brian had the legal right to disconnect the respirator himself, though anyone else's involvement was legally problematic. If Brian were to die at home, the coroner said he would be required by state law to perform an inquest. One possible outcome of that inquest could be prosecution of the assisting physician for homicide.

Burnett explained that because the state of South Carolina does not recognize assisted suicide as a cause of death, he was legally bound to one of two findings: either the patient died of natural causes, or he was murdered.

Personally, the coroner expressed sympathy for Brian's plight, saying anyone "should have the right to discontinue" life support. Rather than discouraging the doctor from carrying out the procedure as Fogarty charged, Burnett says he recommended a process designed to fulfill the statutory requirements of a natural death while protecting Fogarty from possible prosecution. That process would include evaluation of the patient's mental state, obtaining a second corroborating opinion from another physician, and removal of life support within the "controlled environment" of a medical facility.

Curiously, these are the very steps Fogarty would later pursue, though he attributed the inspiration to another source. In any event, Fogarty advised the family to postpone the procedure temporarily pending a legal assessment of the case.

"Now, Brian, I know this isn't what you want to hear," said Fogarty, carefully prefacing his remarks. "But under the circumstances, I think it would be wise to wait until we have a plan in place."

"How long will it take?" Brian asked impatiently.

"I can't really say. Again, I know this is not what you want. But we need to do this the right way."

While the doctor reiterated his support, it did not lessen Brian's disappointment. He was angry and frustrated with a delay that made it unlikely he would meet his August 27 deadline and left him suspicious that legal authorities were positioning themselves to scuttle his plan to die.

The question occurs: Why did Brian need the cooperation of a physician or the sanction of the legal establishment? People voluntarily die each day without either. But complicating matters in this case was the patient's inability to effect his own death. Paralysis had seen to that. Still, there was nothing to prevent him from asking Barbara to disconnect him from life support. However, such a plan was easier to execute in theory than reality.

For one thing, ever since the crisis at the hospital, Brian had lived in chronic fear of suffocation. Though firm in his resolve to die and be done with it, he was equally adamant that there be no replay of the panic he endured that night in the NICU when he first experienced the sensation of suffocation. That recollection reinforced his determination to dictate the time, place, and circumstances of his demise.

For another thing, Barbara was the only possible person he could impose upon to assist him, and he was not prepared to place his mother, who had struggled so mightily with his decision, in the position of serving as his executioner. Barbara admits she sometimes secretly entertained thoughts of personally relieving Brian of his suffering. But she invariably dismissed the notion because she could not bear the thought of assuming responsibility for his death. Consequently, the most viable option available to him was to recruit a physician accustomed to carrying out the task of terminating life support.

The law, with its deference to legal precedents, was rather vague when it came to interpreting this case. Brian's petition should not be confused with the assisted suicides carried out with such notoriety by Dr. Jack Kevorkian. The distinction proved to be a crucial one, since invasive procedures that are the designated cause of death represent a clear violation of statutory law and current medical ethics. In contrast, Brian was asking to be removed from life support, a procedure performed by doctors in hospitals every day. Ordinarily, however, the decision to terminate is made by families in consultation with the attending physician on behalf of unconscious patients, whose deaths are regarded as imminent. Doctors have historically assumed this responsibility because withdrawing life support may hasten death but cannot be construed as causing it.

In Brian's case, however, the patient was conscious, mentally competent, free of any immediate life-threatening condition, and, what's more, he was personally lobbying for the right to die. All of these factors added layers of legal and ethical complexity. Coupling this with the prevailing conservative political climate of South Carolina meant a favorable outcome could not be guaranteed. Fogarty wisely cautioned patience as the issue snaked its way through the legal process. But this was no consolation to Brian, who left the office that night bitterly disappointed.

At another time, Barbara may have looked to her Catholic church for encouragement and support. Early on, when Brian was in rehab in Atlanta and then upon his return to Spartanburg, church members had rallied to the family's aid with financial assistance, visits, and prayers. She was especially close to Father Chris, the founding priest of the parish, who one member lionized as "charismatic, enthusiastic, ecumenical, accepting, dynamic, and caring." Barbara had developed a close rapport with the priest. She considered him a good friend, who offered her a confidential ear and unconditional positive regard.

But Father Chris was transferred to another parish just before Brian's accident occurred. Father Tim, the priest with the misfortune of succeeding this popular figure, turned out to be his temperamental opposite. Already grieving the departure of their beloved priest, some parishioners seized upon the differences in personality and made the new priest the foil for their unhappiness. The conflict that erupted sapped the parish's organizational energy that might have been directed toward the Bacos and other worthwhile causes.

Following the accident, Father Tim made a few obligatory calls on the family, but there was no established relationship upon which Barbara could draw. Preoccupied with defending himself against personal attacks, the priest's interest never developed into any meaningful, sustainable association with the family.

The alienation with the church was symptomatic of what was going on elsewhere. Preoccupied with Brian's care, Barbara was unable to take care of such mundane tasks as mowing the lawn. The grass grew stalks and went to seed, serving as a visual metaphor for the family's hemorrhaging relationship with the community.

Barbara points out that she would have gladly mowed the lawn if someone had volunteered to sit with Brian. But such help was seldom offered. At the same time, she admits to a strong reluctance to ask for help, having grown increasingly self-conscious of imposing upon others in the face of such relentless needs. For her, it actually felt less awkward approaching strangers, like the membership of the Unitarian Universalist Church, than to go begging again to neighbors and friends.

On his return to Spartanburg following rehabilitation, the community had entered into an unwritten social contract with Brian. By word and deed, family, friends, and even strangers communicated: Brian, we value you, and we want you to continue to live among us. If you will give a good effort to survive, we will provide you with the resources you need to have a life worth living.

For a time we delivered on that pledge, and, not surprisingly, it coincided with the period when Brian seemed to thrive. But in subsequent years, the contract was repeatedly violated. It was violated by Herman, Elizabeth, Dean, members of the family, neighbors, friends, many of the private duty nurses, the church, and even the community at large, who despite broad smiles and best wishes failed in the end to deliver on its terms.

Finding himself unable to bear the possibility of his friend confined to a nursing home, Mike considered moving Brian into his own home. But the gesture, while noble, would likely not have produced any more satisfactory results. No one, not Mike or Barbara or any other single individual, could reasonably expect to succeed by taking on such a daunting task alone. The Spartanburg community had it right in the beginning: Brian's well-being could only be ensured by a collective response. Unfortunately, the initial generosity and public support lost momentum and never evolved into a sustainable commitment on which the family could rely.

Richard Mouzon, an Atlanta rehabilitative psychologist who specializes in working with disabled clients, was associated for many years with Shepherd Center. Richard was also a close friend of the late disability activist Dave Webb. Denny Webb asked Richard to consult on the lawsuit against Brian's doctors and to serve as an expert witness in that case. In this role, he interviewed Brian on two occasions and shared the impression of most everyone that Brian was a bright, personable, and hopeful young man.

Richard's involvement in the case was informed by his own disability—a C4-5 level spinal cord injury sustained in an automobile accident at nineteen. The injury short-circuited his plans at the time to become an attorney and drew him instead into the field of psychology, where he continues to be driven by a vision of a more humane world for patients with spinal cord injuries than the one into which he was first introduced back in 1966.

Denny asked Richard to testify in the trial both for his professional expertise and to provide a visual contrast between the respective level of functioning of C4-5 and C2-3 level injuries. Not only does Richard have a busy professional practice, he holds three earned graduate degrees and is married. But he readily admits, "Brian had a rougher road to hoe than I did."

Having lived for much of his life as an incomplete quadriplegic and counseled many others with disabilities, his approach to that life is decidedly unsentimental. He scorns what he calls "the motivational bullshit" and predicts, "without an inspirational ending, no one will buy your book; like at the end of a TV show, you have to catch the robber."

Furthermore, Richard contends that the "job of the disabled person is to help the able-bodied person to feel good about his being disabled." He relates a case on which he consulted at Shepherd where the staff complained repeatedly about a highly antagonistic patient. Richard was retained to provide help for the woman, with the expectation that she would become more compliant.

After conducting an interview and assessing her condition, he concluded that the hostility she exhibited, although disturbing to staff, was in fact an appropriate and healthy expression of her grief. He audaciously proposed that rather than the patient accommodating the staff, the staff be provided training to increase their sensitivity to a patient who was suffering acutely the losses associated with her disability. He says the staff resented his presumption about how they should do their jobs as well as his defense of a patient they expected him to fix. His candor may explain why he seldom receives consultations from Shepherd anymore.

But Richard, peering at the situation through his own eyes of disability, could see what the staff and perhaps the world are largely blind to: a severe spinal cord injury exacts a psychological price from its victims that can be as crippling as the physical impairment itself. As these patients struggle to accept the inherent unfairness of their condition, they are prone to intense emotional eruptions of hostility, rage, and despair that are likely to offend the sensibilities of those around them.

Richard's challenge that the institution adapt itself to the emotional needs of the patient is radical. The able-bodied world scorns such impudence. And the disabled population, sensitive to the subtle cues upon which their very survival depends, swears their oaths of silence, suppresses unacceptable thoughts and feelings, and languishes in anonymity. Occasionally, someone may dare to be insubordinate, like the amputee Richard describes who took to wearing cut-off blue jeans to show off his prosthesis. But by and large, says Richard, disabled people live by the culture's unspoken dictum: "We don't want you begging and looking stupid and silly out there."

He goes on to describe a phenomenon that he refers to as the "rule of infirmity." According to this theory, a patient who is seriously ill or injured can initially expect to receive unconditional support and solidarity from family and friends. But he observes that their support is time-sensitive. If the illness or injury becomes prolonged and the patient does not move visibly in the direction of recovery, those caregivers will soon grow frustrated and impatient. The unspoken message is, "you must recover and you must recover quickly," says Richard.

After two weeks or so of convalescence, patients who have failed to show sufficient signs of progress are demoted to what he calls the "deviant status." One consequence he has observed is the gradual withdrawal of emotional and/or physical support from the patient.

Dr. McCorkle, who by his own admission had no specific knowledge of the rehabilitation program at Shepherd, was anxious to "get Brian up and get him going," so he could "turf" him to Atlanta, a practice in medicine where doctors transfer difficult cases to more specialized care. Shepherd unconditionally released him at the end of his stay there without the benefit of a supervised maintenance program.

The Spartanburg community, so generous in its initial response, eventually ran short of stamina and focus. At every juncture, breakdowns occurred in the continuity of care that denied the reality that patients with high-level quadriplegia never recover. Brian's supporters committed to run a 100-meter dash with him, only to later discover they had signed on for a marathon.

Chapter 32

D r. Fogarty, a rather eccentric man with a strong distaste for the
health insurance industry, is candid in his assessment of his
patient's case. He had the advantage of knowing Brian prior to his
accident when children from the two families competed together in
swim meets. In his characteristically straightforward style, Fogarty
describes Brian's diving accident: "He had a tragic misjudgment and
paid a tragic price for it, which we probably made worse."

He contends that his profession's shortcomings revealed themselves
in at least two specific ways. First, he contends Brian's wishes were
ignored during the time he was a minor. Fogarty first recalls his patient
privately expressing despair with his life and a desire to die at the age
of sixteen. "The health care system would not accept his request much
earlier than eighteen or twenty that we [not] keep him on the
ventilator," he says. "An eighty-year-old with a living will would not
have been expected to appear before an ethics committee."

While many would take exception to his challenge to state law
denying minors the right to self-determination, he does raise some
provocative questions about the condescension his patient experienced
repeatedly at the hands of his health care providers. Ironically, Brian
ultimately returned as a twenty-three-year-old adult to the same
conclusion he had first reached as a teenager—he did not wish to live
with quadriplegia.

Fogarty's other argument acknowledges that Brian was besieged by external, though often unspoken, public pressure to survive. As he explains it, the plot unfolded something like this: "The system gives him help he hasn't asked for. The system gives him no choice. The system says trust us, you'll get better. We'll rehabilitate you.

"Hang in there. You don't know what you're saying. Time goes by, the system has invested thousands of hours and hundreds of thousands of dollars. The unspoken message: How dare you reject my investment in you. . .If he has any sensitivity he realizes that to say no makes him a jerk. He already feels like a jerk living each day with the memory of what he's done to himself and the trouble he's caused his mother and others. . ."

The snare was cleverly designed—trapping Brian in a non-negotiable position where he either had to reject his obligation to others or himself. The decision to die, as Fogarty points out, left those who invested their time and energy in saving his life to feel like fools.

Shepherd Center, while cooperating with me on this book, has seemed anxious about my presentation of this case. Perhaps their apprehension reflects a fear that one patient's maladjustment might somehow discredit many years of work on behalf of spinal cord patients. But at a deeper level it may raise certain fundamental questions about the value of an individual life and the massive industry we have devised to preserve it.

Rehabilitation, according to Fogarty, is a high-stakes game, with reputations, job satisfaction, public image, and institutional survival all dependent on the perception of producing happy, well-adjusted former patients. Shepherd Center's quarterly publication, *Spinal Column*, is a mouthpiece for promoting the accomplishments of that organization. A handful of issues I glanced at profiled former patients who have supposedly graduated to successful, fulfilling lives. Yet nowhere did I read about the struggles of former patients with high-level quadriplegia like Brian. The perennial challenge for the public relations department is to take misfortune and transform it into a more palatable form for staff, patients, and especially donors and prospective donors. As a Shepherd staff person candidly admitted to me, "No one wants to be associated with a failure."

Her comment infers that any individual who chooses not to live with his or her impairment is judged an institutional embarrassment. When asked to consider the plausibility of human suffering that might be irredeemable, Dr. Apple, the longtime medical director at Shepherd, referred to a former patient who wanted desperately to die, only to reverse that position following relocation to a community with more accessible services. The insinuation is that a change of venue may have had the same effect on Brian.

Fogarty compares his patient to a rebellious teen being lectured by the medical establishment: "You're going to enjoy this prom, this life. It is not OK for [you] to say 'no, I don't want to go.' "

The doctor readily admits that survival at any cost is not the solution for everyone, and society must be prepared to accept a patient's personal decision to reject treatment. Furthermore, Fogarty contends Brian faced a community aligned against him, one that insisted he prevail and increased the hardship he experienced in fulfilling his plan to let go.

Some expressed shock when told of Brian's despair. Yet given the plainly miserable circumstances of his existence, one is left to wonder whether these people were truly uninformed or simply chose not to see.

Deborah Seay describes the last year of Brian's life as "unhappy." She watched daily as his strong veneer was absorbed by inner turmoil over an uncertain future. The two of them shared intimate conversations in which he spoke openly of his wish to die and inquired whether she had ever contemplated suicide. He disclosed his plan to terminate his life by having someone disconnect the respirator or by dislodging the tube himself by grasping it between his chin and neck. More than once he asked Deborah to do it for him. It was one request she could not honor, but the fact that he asked spoke to the respect she showed for his feelings and the confidence he had she would not try to change his mind.

In contrast, after learning of his plan, a distraught Mike challenged Brian to prove to him that this was indeed what he wanted. While Mike acknowledged the pressure upon his friend to survive as the community's "symbol of perseverance," he could not abide Brian's decision to die.

In essence, Brian was defying a deeply entrenched cultural value that defends life, no matter how desolate, as always worth living. It is by this premise that capital punishment supporters presume that the death penalty is a harsher sentence than life in prison without parole. And it also informs the wishes of families who insist their relatives with a terminal disease be resuscitated.

Some wrestled with Brian's decision on moral grounds, although, as I would later learn, his request was not inconsistent with Catholic doctrine. The church makes exception when medical care is perceived as requiring "extraordinary means" to sustain life. In such instances, the passive withdrawal of life support is sanctioned.

However, Mike, who had grown up in the same parish as the Baco children, failed to appreciate the ethical nuances. Harkening back to the catechetical training of his youth, he cites the church's historic opposition to euthanasia and defense of the sanctity of life. For devout members of the parish, Brian's decision challenged the unambiguous moorings of their faith that conflict with a technologically changing world.

Brian's predicament was further complicated by his youth. People were prone to object to his decision because they were fixated on length of life rather than its quality.

Brian's friend, Diane, tells of a private conversation she shared with him in the shade of his favorite tree on White Oak Street.

"I don't talk about it much, but my life sucks," he confided in her. "This is hard on my mom, too. I've reached a point where I really don't want to go on."

"Brian, what do you mean?" she said incredulously. "You've got your whole life in front of you."

He could only laugh out loud at her preposterous reply. Again and again, people were unprepared to hear his truth that there are circumstances under which an individual may conclude life is not worth living. Brian struggled valiantly to honor the will of the community, but for once, he was determined to do what he needed for himself. In the end, the will to die in the face of those who did not understand would require as much courage as the act of dying itself.

There is never a time when someone as impaired as Brian resumes a "normal" life cycle as one would following recovery from a broken leg. In fact, there is nothing normal at all about a spinal cord injury. It is an existence predicated upon deprivation more than inspiration. Even one with the self-professed "zest for life" of Richard Mouzon (a disabled person with a lot more personal freedom than Brian) admits to at least three occasions since his accident when he wished to die.

"If I were to express what it's really like [to live with quadriplegia]," he confesses, "it just might cause me not to thrive anymore." He acknowledges that a key to his survival has been an enduring obsession with proving himself by outperforming able-bodied people.

Having divested himself of virtually everything short of subsistence so as not to inconvenience anyone and at the threshold of being shipped off to an institutional warehouse for the duration of his life, Brian was fulfilling the disabled person's oath of invisibility. Everything was proceeding as the able-bodied world dictated until he announced his intention to die. By submitting to death he was, in essence, rejecting submission to something he judged to be far worse, the desperately substandard existence being imposed upon him.

His appeal for the right to die was destined to spark controversy and to evoke plenty of guilt, remorse, and anger in the very people who had joined ranks to form his support system. Acknowledging the dilemma in which Brian found himself, Richard raises the provocative question, "I'm sure people tried to coerce him to live, but did anyone put up any money to keep him there?"

In demanding the right to self-determination, Brian was set to clash with the views of some religious groups, disability rights activists, medical professionals, friends, family, and others who had invested energy and capital in his life. He genuinely feared that some well-meaning person might rush in at the last moment to thwart his plan. Brian was also concerned that the local media might exploit the issue for the sake of sensationalism.

Lacking the energy to counter potentially negative public attention, he largely kept the decision to himself. He was not on a crusade, nor was he trying to make a point. He simply sought the right to dispose of his life with dignity and in privacy. Barbara and I were asked to keep his confidence, which we did. Others, including his closest friends David and Mike, were excluded for reasons that would become apparent later.

In retrospect, Linda Ashley says she can see that Brian's decision to die marked a turning point in her relationship with the family. She became aware of subtle cues she was less welcome in the family's home. Though she continued to send cards and to call periodically, whenever Linda, whose bubbly personality had always made her a family favorite, tried to schedule a visit, Barbara made excuses to turn her away. The signals suggested that an invisible wall was being erected around the Baco compound, effectively shutting the world out.

Chapter 33

For his part, Dr. Fogarty was true to his word. Philosophically predisposed to honor his patient's wish and sufficiently well connected to lead interference, he contacted attorney Steve Williams with the South Carolina Medical Association.

After reviewing the case, Williams proposed a course of action to protect the physician from possible prosecution for his participation in terminating Brian's life support. It included the following:

1. Document a living will for the patient.
2. Document the patient's mental competence by a psychiatrist.
3. Arrange for the hospital's ethics committee to review the case and interview the patient.
4. Invite the state Attorney General to review the patient's living will and give counsel on its legality.

Ironically, the first three steps of Williams' strategy were completed by August 27, the very date Brian had set for his death.

Barbara signed the living will as a proxy for her son, stating his desire that "no life-sustaining procedures be used to prolong my dying . . ." Brian was then interviewed by Dr. Kenneth Wells, a psychiatrist in private practice in Spartanburg. After evaluating the patient, Wells determined: "Brian Bako (sic) in my opinion is not depressed, he is not psychotic, nor does he show impaired cognitive functioning. He is rational in the basis for his request of withdrawal of ventilator treatment. He is fully aware of the consequences of this. He appears to have explored his thoughts and feelings thoroughly both through introspection and in discussion with his mother. Brian Bako (sic) is mentally competent to make any decision on his behalf."

That momentous day concluded with an appearance before the ethics committee of Spartanburg Regional Medical Center. The committee, comprised of physicians, nurses, social workers, attorneys, hospital personnel, and chaired by Chaplain Todd Walter, was asked to rule on the patient's request for self-determination. Brian was irked by having to jump through these institutional hoops. But Fogarty's instincts and Williams' calculations had proven correct. After interviewing the patient and his mother and reviewing reports from Fogarty and Wells recommending consent, the committee "reached consensus to support the expressed preference of the patient to have ventilator support withdrawn."

Fogarty contends, although not all physicians agree, that Brian's diabetes simplified the committee's deliberations. He says the onset of the disease further compromised his prospects for long-term survival and, consequently, strengthened the argument to allow him to die.

All that remained unfinished was authorization from the state Attorney General to honor the patient's living will. But that word did not come at once. Brian waited impatiently as first September and then October came and went.

Around the first of November, another unexpected crisis surfaced. The nursing service, with which the family contracted, announced it would discontinue assignment of its nurses to the Baco residence, explaining the insurance company had failed to reimburse the agency for its services. Rather than continuing to staff the case until the matter could be resolved, the owner of the agency simply cut them off. By the time Fogarty received a response from the Attorney General's office regarding disposition of the living will, Brian was already hospitalized and clearly upset.

"You dumped me here," he said angrily to Barbara.

"What did you want me to do, Brian? I have to work, and I don't have anyone to look after you."

But Brian's mood would soon brighten. According to Fogarty, the Attorney General's office essentially instructed the local coroner to "butt out," clearing a legal path for the patient's living will to be honored. Coroner Burnett says he has no recollection of the Attorney General intervening in the case. But if this was not a turf war, Fogarty questions why the coroner felt it was necessary to alert all area mortuaries to notify his office if they received a body identified as Brian Baco?

Ultimately, Fogarty decided to abandon the plan to withdraw life support in the Bacos' home in favor of the legal protection afforded by the hospital setting. But the hospital administration, fearful of lawsuits, only agreed to participate in the process after first receiving assurance from Barbara that her family would not hold the institution liable. Thus, with an unmistakable poetic symmetry, Brian found himself once again confined to the place where more than seven years earlier his ordeal had begun. Only this time the goal was ending his life, not saving it.

The original plan, as Brian had conceived it, called for the doctor to simply disconnect the life support system, which would result in his death. However, death by asphyxiation, as Fogarty and his partner Wilson Smith appreciated, was a traumatic way to die. Besides the physical discomfort of being starved for air, it was exactly the sensation that terrified Brian most. They were determined, instead, to see to it that his death be as peaceful as possible and, above all, humane.

The doctors first experimented with introducing a different type of respirator that restricted the amount of oxygen Brian's lungs received, theorizing they could gradually wean him of his dependence on the machine. But the reduced flow of oxygen left Brian gasping for breath and was, for him, too closely reminiscent of his near suffocation in the NICU. He quickly vetoed this plan, frustrating Smith, who felt that if the patient was intolerant of the new respirator, maybe he was not ready to die after all.

Another complicating factor for the attending physicians had to do with their patient's condition. Ordinarily, when life support is removed, patients are unconscious, thereby relieving the panic associated with air hunger. With that in mind, Fogarty and Smith formulated an alternative plan that called for Brian to be given an injection of morphine. Once he lapsed into a drug-induced unconsciousness, the respirator could be removed, and Brian would die relieved of any unnecessary discomfort.

In devising this plan, the doctors were cognizant of two factors: First, they wanted to ensure that Brian's death was not traumatic for either him or family members who would witness it. Secondly, he must not die of an overdose. The dose of morphine had to be precisely calibrated to ensure it was potent enough to cause him to lose consciousness without killing him. Some might consider it quibbling in a case where the objective is death, but for Smith, in particular, there was a crucial difference between passive removal of life support and an invasive procedure that precipitates a patient's death. He characterizes the latter as Kevorkian, and for him, it is tantamount to murder. His position is consistent with existing law as well as the Hippocratic Oath by which physicians swear to "give no deadly medicine to anyone if asked nor suggest any such counsel." By careful calibration of the morphine dosage, then, the two doctors intended to induce sleep, not perform an execution.

Despite admitting to the psychiatrist during his evaluation that he had "no real relationship" with his father, Brian's sense of family loyalty and decency prevailed. He informed Herman of his plan to end his life.

Herman still finds his son's fearlessness about death incomprehensible, confessing, "I couldn't do it." But he did not raise any objection, choosing instead to defer to Brian's judgment in the matter. "He was smarter than any of us," he explains. "He knew what he wanted to do. He could handle it, and we were just going to have to handle it."

Others, however, would not have the luxury of time to contemplate Brian's intention to die. As plans were finalized in early November, Barbara began hastily notifying and assembling family and friends to say goodbye. It was impossible to complete such an awkward assignment without offering some explanation to justify her son's decision. Her task was complicated by Brian's insistence on privacy. Uncomfortable with all the sentiment his departure was likely to generate, he fought to keep the event small and manageable.

Excluded from the proceedings were former girlfriend Elizabeth Balaram and friends who had been largely absent from his life since the night of the accident. They would not learn of his decision until after his death.

Some would be hurt by the snub. So be it. For years, Brian had coddled the sensibilities of others. Now, at the end of his life, he was determined to leave this world under his own terms. And in classic Brian Baco style, there would be no dramatic farewells or last rites or final interviews. Brian would handle the last day of his earthly existence with the same quiet dignity that had characterized most of the long years of his disability. Local journalists could bay at the door hoping for a scoop. But barricaded safely within the confines of the hospital, Brian and his family were determined to keep his demise a private, dignified affair.

That Monday night, November 1, Barbara called David at his home in Virginia to tell him of Brian's decision. David recalls sobbing for a long time before he could collect himself sufficiently to prepare for the long drive home. He left from work the next day and drove straight through to Spartanburg Regional Medical Center. A drive he usually made in five hours, this time took only four. He was intent on spending the last two days of Brian's life at his side.

Mike was stricken with disbelief when his phone call came. He was furious with Brian that a decision of such significance could be made without any apparent regard for his feelings. He was equally hurt to be excluded from the inner circle of individuals whose counsel Brian had sought and to be informed of the decision by someone other than Brian himself.

Brian disclosed to the psychiatrist that he had first begun to formulate his plan to die in the fall of 1992. At that time, he had broached the subject of his rights with Fogarty, but it would be the following summer before the plan was presented to his mother, and months more before he told his father and other family members.

It seems he had seriously miscalculated the impact his decision would have. David acknowledges that contemplating Brian's death meant losing "the best friend in the world." Mike, on the other hand, summarized his feelings of betrayal in this way: "Brian was an important part of my life, and it was kind of like he was taking part of my life away from me."

Generous in the attention he lavished upon his friends, Brian had also proven capable of shutting people out. What he was unprepared to share of himself in those final days was destined to haunt those who loved him long after he was gone.

On Wednesday, November 3, he was examined by Dr. E. H. Godfrey, who was asked to give a second opinion in the case. After completing his examination, Godfrey signed a sworn statement which read: "In my opinion, Brian's condition is incurable and irreversible and, in my reasonable medical judgment, would cause his death within a reasonably short period of time if the ventilator, the life-sustaining procedure currently being utilized, is not used."

Wilson Smith signed an identical statement certifying the same. On that same date, Barbara signed and had notarized a declaration swearing that Brian had not requested his living will be revoked. With that, all of the legal conditions had been met.

Chapter 34

November 3, the last night of Brian Baco's life, took on the character of a boys' night out. David, Mike, and Herman all assembled in Brian's room in the post-intensive care unit of the hospital for an evening David would later describe as wrought with "emotional oscillations."

They ordered takeout from Red Lobster and rented some low-budget, sci-fi movies that they pelted with derisive remarks as they watched. But the real agenda had to do with saying goodbye. David compared it to an Irish wake that alternated between moments that were outrageously absurd and others that verged on the incomprehensibly poignant. Only in this case, the deceased, or rather, soon-to-be-deceased, was an active participant.

With his anger beginning to subside, Mike pressed his friend, determined to understand a decision that shook him to his core.

"I'm having a hard time with this," Mike admitted to his friend. "I need to understand why you're doing this."

"It's like this, Mike," Brian explained. "I've always been a big believer in the future, that the future was full of promise. But it's not that way anymore. My life is getting worse and worse. I don't really have anything to live for anymore. If you lose your hope, what have you got?"

Ruby Craig recalls how early on in his disability Brian eagerly awaited reports from the Miami Project, a well-financed, high-profile research effort aggressively working to reverse the effects of spinal cord injuries. But as the years passed and word of the promised miracle cure failed to materialize, Brian's hopes in the project, like those for his own prospects, dimmed.

The report from the psychiatric evaluation probably best captures his mental state at the end of his life. The psychiatrist quotes Brian as saying, "that I have looked at what I get out of life versus what I put in. After seven years, I don't want to go on. It is not one thing but thousands of things."

Brian admitted to Mike that he wanted to believe in a reality greater than human existence, but he could find no evidence to support such a belief. "Maybe there's nothing out there," he explained to his friend, "but it's still better than what I have now."

Herman had questions of his own to ask. Mike sensed that beneath the elder Baco's questioning was a guilt-ridden father hoping to reconcile his unexplained absences while there was still time. Brian, who was well acquainted with his father's ways, treated Herman gently.

Witnesses to the last twenty-four hours of Brian Baco's life were struck by the calmness he displayed compared with the anxiety churning inside them. Greg Lynch compared those final hours to waiting for an "execution."

Brian's serenity appeared genuine, the product of many years of preparing himself for just this moment. In a society so dedicated to resisting death, being in the presence of one serenely prepared to surrender to it can be a mystifying occurrence. None of us keeping vigil at his bedside that night could comprehend that every last hardship he had endured in those seven years was a rehearsal for this one final act of letting go. What we saw was no mirage. Brian Baco really was tough and strong and brave, braced for death by all the renunciations in his life that had preceded it. His poise spilled over and empowered others to reconcile themselves to his decision.

Mike recalls his friend as a rock of stability, even as others around him, including members of the professional staff, appeared shaken. With a maturity that defied his age, Brian inspired others by the calm self-assurance with which he approached the end of his life. His seven years of deliberation over the issue gave him a depth of understanding about the limitations of human existence that those around him were mostly unprepared to consider. Brian became, for all practical purposes, our instructor. When psychiatrist Wells inquired as to why he chose to approach the issue of his death with such directness, he replied, "I want to make it easier for people in the future who have problems like mine."

Drs. Fogarty and Smith are men of strikingly different temperaments. Fogarty, with his aloof, analytical manner, seems the more stereotypical of the two physicians. Conversely, Smith seems a gentle, vulnerable soul.

It was Fogarty who had pursued a legal compromise on behalf of Brian, and it was Fogarty who was recognized as the physician of record in the case. He was the partner with the established relationship with the family, as well as the sole reason the practice was involved in the case at all. Of the two partners, it was Fogarty who was clearest in his defense of Brian's right to die.

For Dr. Wilson Smith, participation in this procedure represented a grave departure from the way he ordinarily practices medicine. In the conventional world of medical science, healing is narrowly defined and does not readily embrace death as a desirable outcome. It would prove to be one of the hardest decisions of the doctor's professional life to lay down that paradigm in order to grant Brian's wish for self-determination. He wrestled with his personal discomfort for all of that week, choking on a concession that for him was a bitter and disagreeable pill. But in the end, he agreed to be responsible for removing life support, a change of heart he attributes to the tranquility and clarity exhibited by his patient. Brian was indeed clear about what he wanted.

When I asked Fogarty why he was absent on an occasion he had worked to make possible, he dismissed it as a coincidence of the partners' respective on-call schedules. But when I posed the same question to Smith, he contradicted his colleague, explaining the duty fell to him because he did not share Fogarty's ties to the patient and his family. The inference is that Fogarty felt too emotionally involved in the case to carry out Brian's wishes. Barbara acknowledges that she observed a visible change that softened Fogarty's professional demeanor after Brian declared his intention to die. She speculates that Brian's struggle to die with dignity "touched something in [Fogarty] he believed in."

Over the course of those seven distressing years, a bond formed between physicians and patient. Fogarty and Smith even made occasional house calls to the Baco residence, an anachronism virtually unheard of today. Brian and Barbara grew to trust them and rely upon their counsel. When Brian became serious about planning his death, it was in Fogarty that he confided. In return, the two physicians developed an intimate appreciation for their patient's condition that Smith characterized as "a living hell." When asked, each could tick off a list of hardships the family endured, from cancellation of insurance to an inadequate support system. It was empathy that animated their determination to honor Brian's wish for self-determination in his death. And it was empathy that revealed itself in the care with which they planned a procedure that would not cause undue anguish for either their patient or his family.

Empathy was a quality often sorely lacking in the medical care Brian received. From the nurse asleep in the next room to the doctor callously exposing his nude body in the presence of visitors, the health care system took the suffering of Brian Baco and aggravated it, often to an unnecessary degree. But in Smith's struggle to lay down his personal discomfort for the sake of his patient and Fogarty's crusade to uphold his patient's wishes, the medical community partially redeemed itself in the end.

Chapter 35a

Barbara called to tell me Brian was scheduled to be removed from life support at approximately 11:00 p.m. that Thursday evening. I agreed to join family and friends already assembled at the hospital. As I hurriedly dressed for the drive to Spartanburg Regional, a lump formed in my throat. I, along with family, friends, and medical staff, was about to witness an extraordinary, life-changing event.

The large number of people that had gathered in Brian's room spilled out into the passageway adjacent to the nurse's station. Special care units do not usually permit such assemblages of people out of respect for the serious condition of the patients they must care for. But this was clearly an unusual set of circumstances deserving of special consideration.

Barbara greeted me at the door of Brian's room and introduced me to a collection of people seated or standing around his bed. I was immediately struck by a lightness of spirit that seemed to defy the grim reality that had brought us all together. Someone would relate a humorous anecdote, which was followed by bursts of laughter. Once, the sound reached such a loud volume that a nurse came to the door asking that we keep it down out of deference for other patients in the unit.

Conversely, the chatter was periodically interrupted by silent pauses when the full gravity of the occasion bore down upon our collective consciousness. Perhaps David's analogy to an Irish wake was a fitting one. The gathering reminded me of the Southern post-funeral ritual I have experienced so often as a minister, where friends and family gather in the home of the bereaved to break bread and decompress their heavy hearts.

The setting in the hospital room was also astonishing for its intermingling of the real with the surreal. This young man, who was admired by so many, would, in just a matter of minutes, be gone from us. Whatever needed to be said or committed to memory, there would only be those precious moments for it and no more. We were groping, all of us, for direction through an unfamiliar territory without the benefit of a map or instructional guide.

I was reminded of the old woman in Voltaire's *Candide*, who, having been ravaged by life's cruelty, confesses: "I've wanted to kill myself a hundred times, but I still love life. That ridiculous weakness is perhaps one of our most pernicious inclinations. What could be more stupid than to persist in carrying a burden that we constantly want to cast off, to hold our existence in horror, yet cling to it nonetheless, to fondle the serpent that devours us, until it has eaten our heart?"

Brian had existed in that very tension of the old woman's musings for more than seven years, loving life dearly yet looking on as it devoured him. The calmness he displayed that last hour of his life was indicative of one who had already surrendered to a superior force. Death was inevitable. Why resist its dominion any longer? There was an abandon in his demeanor that was neither cocky nor cavalier. He was afraid, yet it was not a fear that would keep him from his destiny. His determined calm was infectious. Because he was sure of what he was doing, we could be, too.

The nurse appeared again at the door to announce the doctor had arrived. Taking this as their cue, one by one loved ones stepped forward to bid Brian farewell. As Greg Lynch bent over the bed to say goodbye, Brian whispered a plea that Greg look after Barbara. Most of the group then moved to the waiting room outside the unit.

Only a handful of us remained behind to witness this remarkable event in person. Conspicuously absent was Herman, who was suffering the scorn of the absentee parent. Barbara, who was bitter toward her former spouse for his sudden reappearance after years of neglect, treated him contemptuously. Sensing he was not welcome, he crept off with other relatives to the safety of the nearby waiting room.

But Brian, who knew his old man well and saw through his retreat, had no intention of letting him off so easily this time. Upon learning of his disappearance, he sent Greg with specific orders to retrieve him. Herman at first expressed reluctance but after some gentle coaxing from Greg agreed to return to his son's room. But rather than joining the rest of us bedside, he huddled alone in the corner and looked away from something he found unbearably painful to witness.

The hospital room was now configured to represent the dynamics of the Baco family itself, with one parent at the epicenter of things and the other crouched on the periphery. Yet, strangely, there was grace present even in the depth of their alienation. Brian's insistence that Herman take part in this event was confirmation that his father was still his father. And although the best Herman could manage was a perch in the corner, he is emphatic in his recollection that he looked directly into his son's eyes before he lost consciousness.

Dr. Smith entered the room as inconspicuously as he could and quietly set to work. Those of us who were present circled the bed and joined hands, supplicants trembling before a mysterious rite. Barbara placed her hand tenderly upon Brian's cheek. I was struck by her composure in the face of this painful forfeiture of a part of herself. Is there any loss more deeply felt, any catastrophe more dreaded, than the death of one's child? And yet, there was Barbara bravely unflinching at the end of her six-month struggle to let go of what she wanted for the sake of her son. Standing there that night holding her hand reconfirmed my deep conviction that there is no greater act of human love than the courage to let go the object of one's devotion.

The nurse, with tears escaping the corners of her eyes, fingered a syringe loaded with the appropriate dosage of morphine. She injected it into the intravenous tube located at the side of the bed, and the drug began its slow descent down the plastic canal and into Brian's vein.

We watched silently, both anticipating and dreading the onset of its narcotic powers. For me, it was reminiscent of that moment when, buckled in, the roller coaster first lurches forward, and you realize there is no turning back. Brian's eyes served as the barometer of the drug's effect. They began to turn glassy and his eyelids grew heavy. At last, they closed shut only to spring open again moments later like two window shades being released. He smiled faintly and uttered one final Brian Baco-style refrain: "I'm not gone yet." And with that, Brian closed his eyes for good.

With Brian now fully unconscious, Smith carefully reached for the respirator tube and removed it from the opening in his neck. I'm not sure what we were expecting, but death did not arrive instantaneously. For some minutes, Brian's chest heaved intermittently in an involuntary effort to breathe. Despite the complete paralysis of the muscles of his diaphragm, his lungs writhed and contorted themselves as if screaming for oxygen. Smith described it later as the "break point," where the body's instinctive drive to breathe overpowers the forces compelling it not to. He used the analogy of holding one's breath underwater. A swimmer who does so indefinitely will eventually reach a threshold, where the choice is between surfacing for air or drowning.

A kaleidoscope of impressions crossed my mind as I watched this event unfold. I was relieved Brian was unconscious and grateful for the doctors' wisdom in this matter. Occasionally, Brian's eyelids fluttered, and I winced, afraid that he might awaken again. But he didn't, and as far as I or anyone else could tell, there was no evidence of distress.

I also was reminded of those accounts of near-death, where patients later report having had an out-of-body experience. Was Brian suspended above us looking down on the scene? And if he was, what did he make of it? I remember feeling apprehensive after several minutes of his struggle to breathe. How long could this go on? While it seemed prolonged, in actual time the entire process probably lasted about ten minutes. The pauses between each gasp grew progressively longer until they ceased all together.

Smith checked for vital signs, then turned to note the time. It was 11:45 p.m. Brian Baco was dead.

Compared with the years of suffering, Brian's death arrived swiftly and peacefully. Tears flowed as relief spread like tonic across the room. We, the survivors, embraced one another, having just witnessed an extraordinary event, and one unlikely to be repeated in our lives.

Barbara made her way to the nurse, who was now weeping openly, and wrapped her arms around the woman to console her. Greg remembers Dr. Smith looking dejected and regrets that no one in the room thought to thank or comfort him. After all, he had set aside his reluctance to act on Brian's behalf as an agent of final healing.

When the room cleared, Barbara and I stood alone, gazing upon Brian's lifeless body. It was to be the last time she would see her son. Her calm in that moment seemed almost supernatural. There were no tears, nor was she trembling. Having left behind the hysteria with which she first arrived at Spartanburg Regional Medical Center almost seven and a half years earlier, she now quietly exited the hospital and drove herself home, the beneficiary of yet another new life.

Hoping to preclude the coroner's involvement, Smith listed Brian's cause of death as natural, the result of respiratory failure due to quadriplegia and diabetes mellitus.

However, the coroner was to have the final word. After notification of Brian's passing, Burnette assigned one of his subordinates to conduct an investigation into the death. The investigation included sending bodily fluids off to a lab for analysis, adding one final indignity to Brian's body. Ultimately, however, he ruled that the death was accidental due to the diving accident.

While Brian's initial injury may have indeed been an accident, his death was anything but. His wish to die was plainly documented, and the procedure itself carefully conceived and carried out. The coroner's determination to rule on the case still rankles Fogarty, who characterized it as a "Kevorkian-type show," but Burnett defends his actions as his duty as a public official ensuring compliance with the law.

As Brian had requested, the memorial service was a small affair attended by approximately fifty family members and friends. We gathered on November 6 at the Unitarian Universalist Church of Spartanburg. Out of respect for Brian's wishes, great pains were taken to ensure it was a service befitting of his life. There were tears shed that day, but they were interspersed with the humor that was so much an expression of who Brian Baco was in his life.

As the officiant for the service, I asked our church pianist John Gault to personalize the music for the occasion. The selections we settled upon were hardly memorial service standards. They included the theme from *Star Trek* and a song by Guns n' Roses, one of Brian's favorite bands. To everyone's delight, John managed to locate sheet music that he interpreted on the piano with his customary beauty and skill. Knowing smiles appeared on faces across the room as family and friends made the connection to Brian. It was surely the highlight of the service.

I have long since forgotten the eulogy I prepared in Brian's memory. And for some unknown reason, I failed to save a copy of my notes. But if I were to deliver that eulogy again today, I would surely extol his story as a triumph of hope over despair.

Generally, hope is translated in our culture as an optimism that conditions will improve, or it can refer to a belief in an afterlife. For Brian, neither of these was true. His rational mind did not permit him to envision a destination in some faraway Christian heaven. And as his losses mounted, it became clear that he would never recover the promise of his pre-injured state on earth. For Brian, if the concept of hope was to have any significance at all, it had to be understood in less conventional terms. Sitting alone in his backyard warmed by the sun, the idea of death as deliverance began to congeal and take shape.

The human ego revolts at the insinuation the world might carry on seamlessly without us. But seven years of trying to live with high-level quadriplegia and being confined to a respirator had suctioned off every last ounce of ego from Brian's psyche. In truth, Brian had long since abdicated his personal throne at the center of the universe.

Death emerged as his great emancipator. It promised to liberate him from a perpetual imprisonment he abhorred and his mother from the perversity of serving as his jailer. The idea of death did not fill him with despair; instead, it restored his hope. He came to live for death. He sat there in the sun plotting the circumstance of his deliverance right down to the actual date. He longed for it, dreamed of it, counted down the days 'til its arrival.

The peace we observed on his face in those last hours was not some feigned courage. It was instead the serenity of a man who had accepted a reality he could not change—a man who, at long last, had reached his highest and most difficult goal.

Epilogue

More than ten years have passed since Brian's death, and the dozens of interviews I conducted testify that both his living and dying have been profoundly felt. The emotions he aroused in us, with their tassel of raw and ragged strands, still defy arrangement in the pretty bow of a cheerful ending. Each person was left to consider the loss in his or her own individual way.

David Cullen wore a Raiders T-shirt given to him by Brian for years after his friend's death. Ragged and faded with age, he could not bear to let the shirt go. "[Brian] was just a good friend," he says today. "I didn't have many of them. It's just a very deep loss."

David has suffered from mental health problems since college that included a nervous breakdown. In 1990, with the darkness closing in, he took a year's leave from college and returned home to Spartanburg where he took a job at a Lowe's home improvement store. Much of that year is now a blur to him, but he does recall the times he rode his bicycle the ten miles from his parents' home to see Brian. Those visits helped him maintain his sanity.

David is now married and lives in Spartanburg, where he works as a self-employed software engineer. Though he grew up in a home where faith was not practiced, he became a born-again Christian in 1999. The religious moorings, combined with the miracle of psychotropic drugs, have brought his mental illness under control.

Yet the passage of time has not dulled the painful loss of his friend.

Since returning to Spartanburg, he has avoided Barbara and Dean. And he could never bring himself to honor a pledge he made to Mike to meet on each anniversary of Brian's death. In fact, he finds it easier not to think about him at all. "It's very painful to think about him," he says. "I never really got over it. If I had it to do over again, I would have argued vigorously against removing the respirator."

For Mike Burnette, the experience of Brian's death triggered a crisis of faith he describes as "the most confusing time of my life." The rock-solid assurance of his childhood Catholic faith was shaken by the incomprehensibility of Brian's passing.

Mike now does marketing for a small consumer magazine company in Greensboro, North Carolina. He is married and the father of two young children. He admits that the decision to affiliate with a local Episcopal church, where he teaches Sunday school, is mostly for the benefit of his children. "I'm probably more of a Unitarian or Quaker now than anything," he says, noting that people should make up their own minds about what they believe.

He still wonders whether Brian's decision to die "was the right course to take." But he also acknowledges there is no way to know, since he was not in his friend's predicament. Though Mike seems to have made peace with the loss, there remains in the back of his mind one formidable question: "Could I have done more to help Brian stick around and have a viable life? It's something I've never resolved."

Deborah Seay, now Deborah Thompson, was no longer Brian's private duty nurse at the time of his death. After remarrying, she moved to a rural area some fifty miles from Spartanburg. Her goodbyes had been said many months earlier when she told Brian of her plans to resign. Yet at the time of our interview, she still wrestled with guilt feelings that she had abandoned him. She admits Brian was the only patient she served who managed to penetrate her professional veneer. Having established a close bond with him only to lose it, Deborah walked away from the nursing profession vowing never to return again.

In contrast, I found Ruby Craig to be her same irrepressible self, working at two nursing homes while continuing to oversee her multi-generational brood of children. After being discharged by Elizabeth, she maintained contact with Brian by phone for the duration of his life. Although personally disapproving of his decision to die because of his youth and talent, she nevertheless expressed respect for his right to choose.

Dean Baco was conspicuously absent at his brother's death, a fact that was hurtful to Brian. When asked to explain why, Dean would only say that he refused to watch them kill his brother. According to Barbara, her surviving son, who is now thirty, continues to ignore his potential for a life of drugs and legal problems.

Arranging to speak with Elizabeth Simmons, formerly Elizabeth Balaram, was complicated by her family's disapproval and her own reluctance to revisit an unpleasant part of her past. However, she finally agreed to an interview over the objection of both her husband and her parents.

At the appointed time for our interview, I opened the door and beheld a person quite different from the one I had pictured in my head. Wan and almost delicate in appearance, she hardly seemed like the person described to me who had terrorized Brian's family and friends. Perched lightly on the edge of the sofa, she spoke to me bashfully, with her gaze diverted toward the floor.

At the time of the interview, she was working as a nursing assistant with plans to pursue a four-year degree in nursing, a vocation that first occurred to her while caring for Brian. But recollections of events from that period in her life have grown dim, and she showed little interest in resurrecting them. Her one introspective moment that day was the admission that she had rebelled against her parents and unwisely rejected those who offered her help with Brian.

Herman Baco now resides in the Cajun country near Lafayette, Louisiana, where he works in the retail industry. While Barbara spins dark theories about what makes her ex-husband tick, Herman has only kind words to say about her. He also expresses compassion for Dean's troubles: "I still make stupid mistakes. How can I blame someone else?"

As for his elder son, he acknowledges an appreciation of how Brian "saw a life of isolation and desperation stretching out before him."

And unlike his ex-wife, he resisted the urge to intervene in the personal decision to terminate life support.

Barbara remains deeply divided about the man with whom she once shared a life. On one hand she attacks his character with language ordinarily reserved for an archenemy. She speaks disdainfully of his failure to pay the funeral expenses, which delayed by several years her efforts to settle their son's estate. After learning the debt was delinquent, she paid a visit to the funeral director to ask why he had not called. He told her, "'I sat there with you all when Herman said he was going to take care of the funeral charges because you had taken care of Brian. So, I wasn't going to call you.'"

On the other hand, she calmly recalls the "great time" she and her sister enjoyed as guests at his home for Mardi Gras.

And proving that a marriage is easier to dissolve legally than emotionally, when Herman suffered a stroke two years ago, his co-worker found Barbara's phone number in his Palm Pilot and called her. When Herman's family failed to respond to his illness, Barbara took off a week from work and drove down to care for him in the hospital. "There was nobody left but me," she explains.

Barbara says she extended the gesture because Herman is the father of her children, though she also admits she would never do it again. "It was a week of experiencing him all over again," she says. "It was a reminder of why I left him."

For Barbara herself, recovery has been measured in years rather than days or even months. The liberation she had secretly dreamed of for so long did not start out as she had imagined it.

After seven years consumed with keeping Brian alive, she returned from his memorial service to an empty house. The disorientation was enough to send her spiraling into despondency. First diagnosed with clinical depression in 1990, she was prescribed the antidepressant Prozac, which she is convinced only deepened her despair. The switch to another antidepressant, Zoloft, took just enough of the edge off the depression that she managed to save her job. But the medication's effect came at the price of reducing her to what she calls an "unfeeling zombie." When Brian announced his intention to die, Barbara began to wean herself off the medication, determined her son's death would not go unmourned. But the devastation of losing him, combined with her own imbalanced brain chemistry, set her adrift.

"I sometimes feel ashamed," she once confessed, "because the grieving Brian didn't want me to do, I do, and the life he wanted me to have, I don't make an effort to go out and have."

Resentful of individuals she accuses of deserting her and yet barricaded within the walls of her home, she was destined in the first years of her sorrow to recreate familiar patterns of the unloved and unlovable person.

Soon after Brian's death, she went to buy groceries. Once inside the store, she spotted a woman she knew from the Catholic church trying hard to avoid eye contact with her. Barbara grew angrier and angrier as the woman dodged her aisle by aisle all the way across the store.

What peace Barbara has derived from her experience is to be found in the strength of relationship. This woman who can so blithely bemoan, "When in my life have I ever been lucky?" was blessed with a level of intimacy with another human being many people never realize. The love she shared with Brian was transcendent, empowering each of them to survive seemingly unbearable circumstances with their sense of humor and sanity largely intact. Saddled early in life with the rejection of her biological parents, she eventually discovered in relation with her elder son a love that was enduring.

It was, of course, nothing like in the storybooks. When she could not bear to go home at night to deal with the circumstances of his disability, it was to love that she appealed. When all else failed, it was love that sustained her, love that renewed her, and ultimately, love alone that made her wiser and more resilient than she had ever been before.

And when in the end what she wanted most was to hold on tightly, it was love that supplied the strength she needed to let go. It was love that coaxed, prodded, and stretched her into someone new and improved. The hysterical mother in the emergency room the night of the accident was hardly recognizable in the calm, centered person who in the moments following her son's death had the presence to reach out and console another. The two people were different—radically different—as different as the sun is from the moon. And it was love that made all the difference. Neither the might of the insurance industry nor the indifference of the medical establishment could quash it.

When asked in retrospect if the seven years with Brian were worth what it cost her, she responds with an emphatic "Yes." For the sake of Brian Baco, she would indeed do it all again.

Today, thanks to the healing powers of time, Barbara has been revived. Her depression has lifted. Life has returned to the little home on White Oak Street, evidenced by the menagerie of animals including a cockatoo named Coco, a parakeet named Tiki, and three dogs called Bootsie, Silky, and Cricket. But it still seems odd to sit on real furniture and chat with her in the living room once dominated by her son's hospital bed.

After Brian's remains were cremated, Barbara drove to the local mortuary to collect the ashes that were waiting for her in a small box. As a tribute to him, she had ordered a pink dogwood tree to be planted in the backyard. Several friends joined her informally in the backyard one afternoon for a ritual of spreading the ashes at the base of the young tree. One of the participants produced a pair of latex gloves to insulate her hands from the messy work. But not Barbara.

"That was my son," she explains. "Flesh of my flesh and life of my life. And I wasn't going to scatter his ashes with anything on my hands."

The visceral sensation of holding the residue of Brian's life in her bare hands and scattering it in the place that had been his sanctuary proved healing for her. Its first spring, "Brian's Tree," as she refers to it, showed forth spectacularly in delicate pink blossoms that in the Christian tradition symbolize rebirth.

Like Mike Burnette, Barbara's faith has undergone major alterations. Religious clichés and formulas that may have comforted her in the past grew hollow in the face of so many years of seemingly pointless suffering. Barbara, like the Israelites of antiquity, was destined to wander a barren landscape, menaced by loneliness, confusion, and despair. She swears that she has never blamed God for what happened to her son, but the events have left her unsure exactly what to believe.

"Maybe it is all just birth to death; maybe there is nothing else. . .I want to believe that purpose can come out of unfortunate circumstances, but it doesn't help ease my pain," she says.

Barbara's search for answers that do not come is a universal human yearning that insists our days, and particularly our hardships, be infused with some transcendent meaning resplendent with divine purpose and design.

In the summer of 1973, Donald "Dax" Cowart was critically injured and seriously disfigured in a propane gas explosion. Lonnie Kliever collected and published a series of essays comparing Cowart's desire to die with what would prove to be an insurmountable resolve on the part of family, friends, and caregivers that he survive.

Dax's Case examines the concept of "redemptive suffering" whereby societies seek to rescue human misery from its random senselessness. Religions of many cultures attempt to infuse human tragedy with some kind of universal significance so as to offer victims a way through or, at least, around otherwise incomprehensible circumstances. What seems apparent is our general discomfort with suffering that may be irredeemable and the extent to which we will go to deny it.

At its core is a possibility that may be too darkly despairing for many to even contemplate. Plainly put, it is the bold supposition that life itself may have no ultimate meaning. As the existential philosopher Albert Camus once proposed, "There is but one truly serious philosophical problem, and that is suicide."

Camus' remark hardly makes for pleasant dinner conversation, but it may explain the stout resistance Brian Baco encountered on the way to ending his life. Those who, like Brian and Dax, wish to surrender to death present a formidable challenge to our conviction that all life is purposeful. They push us invariably to a place where religion cannot go. It is a place where glib declarations about the sanctity of life fall upon utter silence. If Brian's life was not worth living, then how can I be sure mine is? And if I cannot be sure my existence is the realization of a master plan, then by what authority do I crawl out of bed this morning and meet the day?

It's all rather scary to think about, I know. Most of the time we can insulate ourselves from encounters with the darkness. But then occasionally something happens: for instance, a stupid, senseless accident like the one that befell Brian Baco. And there we are again, peering uncomfortably into that dark, dismal chasm of the unknown.

As I consider how imposing that reality is to us, legal rulings that pronounce all suicide wishes as irrational, and even immodest bumper stickers that declare: "I know God exists. I talked with him (sic) this morning," become more understandable and perhaps even a bit more tolerable.

Brian's story is a compelling illustration of a basic paradox of the human condition. We struggle so mightily against forces over which we exercise so little control. With heroic effort, we may postpone, defer, or temporarily suspend the moment of our individual reckoning, but no matter how grand our schemes, no matter how sophisticated our technology, for each of us that reckoning will arrive. Therefore, the question is not whether we will die but when and how. There is today no reason to submit to death unnecessarily soon as in previous generations, but neither is there any reason to prolong human suffering beyond what is reasonable.

Because of my past professional experience as both a minister and hospital chaplain, it has been my privilege to witness the deaths of many people. I have seen people die from all kinds of causes and at different stages of life, from the very old to the very young.

And after much reflection, I have come to what represents for me two undeniable conclusions, the first being there is nothing very remarkable about death. In opening our eyes, it soon becomes apparent that the material world is founded upon the impermanence of all living things, from the changing of the seasons to the molting of a snake's skin. Likewise, at this very moment, our bodies are sloughing off millions of dead cells to be replaced by new ones that will also eventually die. Death supports life even as life precedes death.

However, we live today in a culture that worships youthful beauty, where death is a morbid topic unfit for polite circles. The taboo against talking about the subject is so strongly inbred and our exposure to death so rare anymore, that it really is possible to reach middle-age and experience the cultural phenomenon we call a mid-life crisis, which is nothing more than an encounter with the fact we are temporary. I am convinced the experience of dying could be made significantly less dreadful and traumatic for everyone if it weren't treated as a horrific and unnatural process.

The second conclusion is that though death may be altogether unremarkable, life itself is spectacularly extraordinary. I sometimes catch myself doing something as seemingly ordinary as flexing my arm to raise a coffee mug to my mouth when I am suddenly struck by the realization that this was something Brian could not do after his accident. What I came to appreciate in his disability is all the myriad of things that could go wrong with the human body that, for most of us, blessedly never do. Something as simple as flexing my arm requires a precise sequencing of unseen processes that make manned space flight to distant planets seem small in comparison.

There is no mystery in the fact we eventually wear out and die. That is plain for the human eye to see. But the fact that we ever live at all—now that is truly mysterious. The single cells that first improbably formed themselves as living organisms millions of years ago out of the primordial ooze continue to this day to be reborn in the hope and promise with which each new generation arrives on this planet.

In my more egotistical moments, I can still imagine myself to be the center of my universe. Yet deep down I know that my tiny individual existence is nothing as compared with this timeless and continuous chain of life. In me resides the cumulative product of those who have gone before as well as the genesis of all who will follow. The realization that we do not live only for ourselves is our one, defiant vote against despair. As Erik Erikson once observed, "If we are not afraid to die, our children will not be afraid to live."

When I appeared before the ethics committee at Shepherd Center to review the case of Brian Baco, I found myself straddling a dichotomy that seems so quintessentially American. The panel was divided between those who were vocal in their support of Brian's right to self-determination and those just as passionately concerned that his decision might help erode the present system that encourages the survival of patients with spinal cord injuries. There were also those who were willing to concede the credibility of both positions.

That committee is a microcosm of our complex society. On many fronts today, from substance abuse to abortion, from education to poverty, we seem torn by the tension between the rights of the individual and the common good. Historically, where other societies have sought to suppress civil rights for the sake of public interest, Americans enthusiastically embrace the constitutional guarantees of individual "life, liberty, and the pursuit of happiness." Consequently, American civic life careens as possibly no other before it in human existence between these two competing, sometimes contrary, interests.

The process of finding a satisfactory middle ground is messy, inefficient, and often unsatisfying, especially for purists. Activists fear that Brian's decision to die starts us down a slippery slope on which disabled people might become as disposable as a lame thoroughbred. Certainly, our national history is less than exemplary when it comes to defending the rights of such minorities.

Yet if we are to be true to our constitutional precepts of protecting the rights of the individual, we cannot summarily dismiss the freedom to choose death over a substandard existence. Just as existing abortion laws allow for women to arrive at radically different decisions regarding an unwanted pregnancy, so Brian's wish to die does not impugn the integrity of millions of other disabled persons who remain committed to living.

I have attempted to analyze the conditions upon which Brian's decision was predicated, but truthfully his death wish first materialized at the bottom of the Lantern Ridge Pool, long before those conditions were known to him. It was a position that he held for much of those seven years he lived with quadriplegia and one from which, in the final analysis, no one was able to dissuade him.

Could marriage, a successful career, more resources, greater community support, or relocation to a new community have changed his mind? We can never know for sure. Perhaps timely intervention would have made a difference, but perhaps not.

According to the American ethos, one person's experience and volition does not necessarily presume that of another. The more relevant question I must ask of myself is: Can I be respectful of another person's personal decision even if it does not square with what I would have done?

Everyone, it seems, from those who want to ban pornography to those who demand we police and punish politically incorrect speech, believes in the First Amendment until bumping into behavior they find personally reprehensible. The real test of our constitutional guarantees of self-determination is the extent to which we are capable of sitting with our personal discomfort in the face of that with which we disagree. As Dr. Fogarty allows: "The health care system is not the solution for everyone. There are times when patients will reject our treatments. We shouldn't make it so difficult for them."

In the case of Brian Baco, there was a perceived public interest to be served. By his survival, Brian was helping to reinforce America's image of itself as a fair and just society. His plight initially appealed to people's sense of decency and altruism. By their contributions to re-establishing his place in the community, residents of Spartanburg could feel they were honoring their civic duty to be neighborly.

What the community was not prepared for, however, was the extent to which Brian would require assistance to lead a satisfactory life. After the initial flurry of help, it was expected that the boy and his family would be restored to relative independence. The situation left Brian caught in a bind between a culture that demanded self-sufficiency of him and a disability that would not permit it.

Yet his story is as much about a system failure as anything. Had Brian and Barbara relocated to the Atlanta area, he could have taken advantage of an assortment of services and programs offered through Shepherd Center. Shepherd has pioneered an intern program through which persons with neurological impairment are paired with local employers. During a three-month trial period of employment, these individuals are given the opportunity to prove themselves competent in the work place. Programs such as this, which cultivate relationships with local businesses and promote the capabilities of disabled people, increase the likelihood of someone in Brian's condition finding work.

A disabled person in the Atlanta area also lobbied for and was granted a government waiver whereby monthly payments to a residential care facility could be transferred to attendant care. Such a waiver would have permitted Brian to continue to live with his mother rather than being confined to a nursing home.

But such options were largely unknown in a small community like Spartanburg. By returning to his hometown, he was set down in an environment unprepared to accommodate someone with his acute level of need. While Shepherd Center has made Atlanta a magnet for individuals with spinal cord injuries, Brian's fate in Spartanburg was to remain a lonely curiosity. Ironically, life in his hometown only intensified his sense of isolation and helplessness.

A member of the Shepherd Center ethics committee wondered aloud why no effort was made to actively intervene on Brian's behalf to improve the circumstances of his life. The question was both provocative and deserving of a response. Why, for example, was the local vocational rehabilitation center not contacted to prepare him for employment? That is, after all, its mission.

Unfortunately, those of us who tried to help were victims of our own feeble ignorance. As a member of the clergy, I had often served as a referral source to people with needs, yet in this case I meekly deferred to Brian's decision without trying to access help for him. I personally failed Brian because of my inexperience with severe disability, lack of knowledge about available services and support, the distractions of my own life, and perhaps, foremost, a reluctance to intrude upon an individual's personal life.

Others failed him for similar reasons. Unwittingly, his decision to die was the one to which collectively we had abandoned him.

As I pause to consider the failure of this system, the image that comes to mind is of the night of Brian's high school prom. I can imagine Barbara and Ruby struggling with his tuxedo, Emily operating the video camera, Linda lending moral support, Herman and Sean providing transportation, Elizabeth at his side beaming with pride, and his friends greeting him warmly upon his arrival at the dance. It was one of the best moments of Brian's seven-year ordeal. No one probably realized it at the time, but our strength was always in our numbers.

As I stood at Brian's bedside that fall evening of 1993, hands joined to those closest to him, I had a keen sense that things were working out as they should, that Brian was at last achieving the fulfillment of the only wish remaining to him—a death of personal choice to supplant a life bereft of any. What others might think, believe, recommend, pray, or plead for at that moment, or since, was of far less significance. The occasion was deeply personal and the result of Brian having devoted those years of incapacitation to working through what it meant to him to be alive. His story is a testimony to the indomitable human spirit that imbued both his life and death with dignity.

Historically, human beings endowed of that same spirit have been greeted each morning, consciously or not, with Camus' universal inquiry and in almost every instance and for no comprehensible reason have decided to plow on through the day. The struggle to live takes a backseat only to the struggle to live meaningfully.